Open Mike: From Corporate Radio to New Media,
The Story of The Mike O'Meara Show

is a Hay Bale Media, LLC Book

Please visit us online at *www.haybalemedia.com.*

Open Mike

*From Corporate Radio to New Media,
The Story of The Mike O'Meara Show*

as told to W. Michael Kelley

TABLE OF CONTENTS

FOREWORD

Mike O'Meara and I first met when we were mere lads in Liverpool, England. He had a band called the Quarrymen, and I saw them playing onstage. Mike was rough around the edges and seemed to be slightly drunk. He was singing something like "Come Go With Me," but he clearly didn't know the words! He was making up his own lyrics! "He's right daft," I thought, but there was still this magnetism. After his set, I introduced myself, and ... wait a minute. That's not right. That's someone else's "how we first met" story. Sorry.

I don't actually remember the first time I met Mike. What I do remember is being "aware" of him. We were both in the Class of 1981 at American University (or, as they used to insist we call it, THE American University). Tuesday nights at the Tavern (I'm sorry, THE Tavern), the on-campus hot spot for drinking and entertainment, were big, busy nights. Most students didn't have class on Wednesdays, so everybody went to the Tavern and got drunk. (I didn't, of course, as I did not—and still don't—drink. I'm serious!)

I remember first being aware of Mike DJing there, spinning records in case people wanted to dance. Which they didn't, much. Mainly they drank. But my vague recollection is of Mike playing the tunes, making wisecracks about some of the people in attendance, and getting drunker as the night went on. I really should ask him if this is what really happened, as I sometimes wonder if I have made this all up in my head, based on what I later knew of Mike. I *should* ask him, as I am a journalist (I think), but for the purposes of this foreword we will just assume my recollections are accurate.

I also have a vague memory of him playing the drums in a band one night at said Tavern, but I'm not sure about that, either.

Anyway, eventually I "met" Mike at WAMU-AM, the student-run college radio station. We both had shows on the air. WAMU was a powerhouse back then, with a signal strength that *almost* allowed everyone on campus to hear it. Again, I'm serious! It must have been broadcasting at two watts, or something, as even just across campus, it would come in equal parts programming and static. But that didn't stop us radio nerds from indulging and developing our love of radio and broadcasting in general. Even then, Mike seemed a larger-than-life figure, completely throwing himself into whatever it was he was doing at any moment: emceeing WAMU's "Radio-thon" for Children's Hospital, arguing about his beloved New England sports teams, or drinking.

Little did any of us know back then what a big star and a force in radio that Mike would become. First, when he teamed up with Don Geronimo at WAVA-FM as one of the nation's first (and most popular) "morning zoo" shows, and later when *The Don and Mike Show* dominated locally and nationally at WJFK-FM, he enjoyed extraordinary success and grew into an incredibly talented and funny broadcaster.

My relationship with Mike always strikes me as funny, because we truly are friends, but at the same time, I am a HUGE fan. I cannot possibly tell you how many times I would be "stuck" in my car or at my desk, glued to *The Don and Mike Show* or, later, *The Mike O'Meara Show*. I could be doubled over in laughter, or, on occasion, moved to tears, depending on what was going on. And the days when Mike and his gang have been kind enough to invite me onto the show? (Or even, on one occasion, fill in for an ailing Mike?) Forget about it! It was like being invited onto Johnny Carson's *Tonight Show*, as far as I'm concerned. It's an honor, and you want to bring your "A" game so that you don't "F" it up!

I kid Mike about a lot; we all do, but it is done with affection. Is he mercurial, prone to sudden anger or irritation? Nope. Not even sure why I brought that up.... (But really, aren't a lot of supremely talented people mercurial?) I do know this: I really admire Mike. I admire his talent, his true love of broadcasting (may it rest in peace), and his loyalty. I don't think he allows himself to think this, but it's true: he has been a trailblazer in radio, and now he is a trailblazer in the world of podcasting. He is, quite simply, one of the best in the business there has ever been.

I'm serious about that, too.

Tony Perkins
Former comedian,
Current news anchor,
WTTG-TV
Washington, D.C.

November 2013

Introduction

Once I'd passed the fourth used tire shop, I knew I was getting close. It was a crisp, bright day in early March, and I was nearing the end of a nearly three-hour drive from my home to Manassas, Virginia—a historic town approximately 30 miles west of Washington, D.C. If you are a history buff, you'll recognize Manassas as the site of the first major land battle of the Civil War, the First Battle of Bull Run, a defining moment in the war.

Of course, the historical significance of the town was utterly lost on me. I knew of Manassas for one reason: it was the hometown of Mike O'Meara, a radio personality I had followed since I was a junior in high school. Over 20 years later, I was just as big a fan as ever, and it seemed surreal that I was going to meet Mike face-to-face. His home also served as the world headquarters and production studio for the newest incarnation of his show, in podcast form.

———

A few months earlier, I contacted Mike about the possibility of working together on a book about him and his show. He called me back within the hour, and we agreed to meet at his home in The Zit—a nickname for Manassas that belies his love-hate (but mostly hate) relationship with the town. It was all happening very quickly, and unfortunately, now that the day was upon me, I was sweating like a stuck pig. I passed another landmark, an intersection at which three of the four corner lots were occupied by drug stores of different chains. "This is the 'historic drugstore district,'" I muttered aloud to no one. Even closer to *The Mike O'Meara Show* studios.

I found the house, circled it a few times to try and settle my nerves, and climbed out of my car. I knew I shouldn't arrive too early, because he was taping an episode that day, and the last thing I wanted to do was disrupt the show. When I reached the front door, I was greeted by a handwritten sign: "Recording in progress. Do not knock or ring the bell." I stood there stupidly for a moment, not sure what to do, until a woman shouted to me from a passing car. "Are you Mike? Go ahead and knock. They're finished taping." It was Carla O'Meara, Mike's wife. After her many appearances on the show, I recognized her voice immediately.

I knocked, and when Mike answered, he immediately put me at ease. "Come on in, brother. Everybody, this is Mike, the author I told you about." I shared a few polite handshakes with the guys on the show, and he led me back to his kitchen. "This is where I do most of my business." He nodded perfunctorily toward a small, furry mound on the floor against the wall, where a plump black pug and a quivering, tan, long-haired Chihuahua were intertwined in a sleepy embrace. "Don't mind the dogs."

———

I explained my vision. We'd collaborate to write a book about *The Mike O'Meara Show*, a story that's more relatable now than ever in an unstable economy. Fans of the show would love more insight into each of the key players, but I wanted the book to have a broader appeal. There were so many depressing stories about people losing their jobs and news articles about the rising unemployment rate that I wanted to share a story with a happy ending. Cast off by terrestrial radio, *The Mike O'Meara Show* returned on its own terms, with its own business model, and showed people that getting fired is not always the dismal end it feels like at the time.

Mike was instantly enthusiastic. "I love this idea," he replied, taking a pull on an electric cigar—a product I recognized as a sponsor of his podcast. "I have two conditions. First, I don't know anything about publishing books, so I will trust you. You won't get any help from me on that end, because I've never done anything like this before. Second, we take the high road on everything. I've had a long career with ups and downs, but I am not about to start bad-mouthing anyone I've ever worked with."

He removed the cigar from his mouth, and for the first time in our meeting, the mirth was gone from his face. "Can I trust you with this? I'm not interested in pursuing this any further unless I believe that you'll take what I am saying seriously. Some people like the bad stuff, the dark underbelly, the gossipy crap. They feed on it, but that's not what I am about, and as long as you're on board with that, we have a deal."

I nodded, and the twinkle returned to his eye. Behind another puff of electronic cigar smoke, he laughed. "But if I wanted to, I could tell you some stories that would curl your hair, that's for sure."

Business concluded, Mike walked me to the front door of his home. As the door opened, we were met with the wailing of a passing fire truck and police cruiser. "You hear that?" he asked, laughing. "It's the Manassas welcome wagon! They're welcoming you to The Zit, brother!"

Most of my research for *Open Mike* was conducted over the phone in one-on-one conversations with the participants. After our conversations, each person was provided with a typed transcript for their review. Everyone involved was so willing to open up to me, even about personal and intimate matters, that I felt obligated to give them the opportunity to recant or redact portions of our conversation. No one did—everything they told me on the record stayed on the record.

The interviews took place over a one-year period of time. Because the book is organized topically, rather than chronologically, occasionally people refer to the same events in the past and in the future. This is most obvious with the birth of Mike's son. Mike speaks of the upcoming birth of his son and his newborn son, because I spoke to him before and after Michael William O'Meara was born.

After I concluded my research, I decided that the book would work best if I let the players speak in their own words. Many of the contributors to the book are professional broadcasters, so paraphrasing them in the third person felt almost blasphemous.

All speakers are credited, so you can assume that I wrote any text not specifically attributed to someone. For a complete list of the individuals quoted in the book, and a brief bio of each person, see Chapter 2. I followed the model set by Tom Shales and James Andrew Miller in their 2002 book *Live From New York*, which cuts together individual interviews to read like one, ongoing conversation. Think of this book as the printed version of a documentary film, which edits together footage shot at different times and at different locations.

That said, if I were to leave the transcripts unmodified, the book would read somewhere along the spectrum where "choppy" is the best case scenario and "feels like I am reading the ramblings of an incomprehensible lunatic" as a worst case. To make the book flow better, and to avoid the whole lunatic worst case, some editing was required. However, no changes were made to alter the tone, message, voice, or intent of the speaker.

Occasionally, the best spokesperson for the show is the show itself, so the book includes some partial transcripts of different *Mike O'Meara Show* podcasts. These are some of my favorite moments of the show, segments that shed light on the show's major players while communicating the voice and tone of the show better than any description I could muster. These transcripts are edited for space and, occasionally, for content.

Finally, fans of the show will notice that while this book focuses on the final days of the show on terrestrial radio at WJFK and the early days of the show as a podcast, it does so through the perspectives of its current broadcasting team: Mike O'Meara, Robb Spewak, and Oscar Santana. This approach provides a comprehensive view of the show's history while honoring Mike's specific instructions not to delve into negatives about the past. "Ever forward," as the guys like to say.

Keep in mind that this book is not a work of investigative journalism. It never intends to embarrass or debase any of its participants nor those of whom they speak. In this modern era of ubiquitous online gossip journalism, you may be expecting salacious details and humiliating secrets. You will find neither here. This book exists to celebrate success snatched from the jaws of failure, to explore more fully an entertainer and his show that have brought joy to millions of people. Like the book *Live From New York* that inspired its form and tone, I have only one goal: to faithfully document the participants in their own words.

To close, I'd like to thank all of the people who helped with this project, including *Mike O'Meara Show* fans Shannon and Michael who provided crucial feedback throughout the entire project. The book is much better because of their participation. I also need to thank my wife, who encouraged me to pursue this project and served as chief of the editorial staff. Every day I get to work with her is a joy for me.

It was my great honor to undertake this project. I spent a year speaking to people I have only heard on the air or watched on television, and any success this book finds is the result of their kindness and willingness to lay themselves bare in print, just as they do on the air every day.

1
THE END

The most pivotal moments in your life rarely play out as you'd expect. In 1985, just four years after graduating from American University in Washington, D.C., a young radio disc jockey named Mike O'Meara partnered with fellow jock Don Geronimo. The duo quickly gelled with their daily *Morning Zoo* radio broadcast on radio station WAVA 105.1 FM. They wove compelling and entertaining stories of their lives between the chart-topping hits of the day, and when they jumped stations to WJFK 106.7 FM in 1991, their fans came with them.

For 17 years on WJFK, *The Don and Mike Show* consistently ranked first in its afternoon time slot. The four-hour daily show was nationally syndicated, boasting millions of listeners from coast to coast who were enamored with their unique style of "shock jock" fare. Don, often the brash "bad cop," was tempered by Mike, the "good cop"—roles they both exaggerated for comedic benefit and long-lasting ratings success. With annual contracts that stretched into seven figures, Don and Mike truly earned the self-proclaimed title of "Radio Gods."

Mike was more than just a voice of balance on the show. He contributed a multitude of voices, spot-on celebrity impressions that were so natural and uncanny that even longtime fans occasionally cocked their heads as they listened, wondering, "Did they actually get Harry Morgan in studio?" His impressions brought Mike national recognition, for a wealth of reasons both good and bad.

In 1998, Jon Stewart was promoting his first book, a collection of essays called *Naked Pictures of Famous People*. He appeared on the *NPR Weekend* radio show with an audio production of a popular essay in the book titled "Adolf Hitler: The Larry King Interview." The premise: Hitler finally "owns up" to all of his despicable actions like any other modern-day celebrity, with an apologetic media tour. When Larry King refused to play himself, Mike O'Meara was tapped to play King opposite Stewart, who played Hitler. The only person more qualified to play Larry King, other than Larry King himself, was Mike O'Meara. The essay was funny, but the recording was hysterical. You have to *hear* Larry King ask, "Annie from Grand Rapids, Michigan, what's your question for Adolf Hitler?" to truly appreciate the deft absurdity of Stewart's writing.

On at least one occasion, Mike's impressions would also land the duo in hot water. *The Don and Mike Show* delighted in tracking down celebrities as they traveled, sleuthing out their hotels and trying to reach them by phone when they least expected it. In 1995, they discovered where Regis Philbin was staying when his show *Live with Regis and Kathy Lee* was taping on location. They left him a number of messages but were not content to leave it at that. Instead, Mike called the hotel, on-air, as Regis Philbin himself, convincing the hotel clerk to play all of "his" voicemail for him. Incredulously, Don and Mike listened to all of Regis' messages, including the messages they had just left. Once was not enough; they did the same thing the next day, again leaving and then retrieving Regis' voicemail live on the air.

Unfortunately for Mike—but fortunately for those who were listening at the time—the final Regis voicemail call ended in spectacular fashion. After asking Mike (as Regis) to hold, the hotel clerk rejoined the call with a perplexing statement: "Mr. Philbin, I have Mr. Philbin on the line." Regis Philbin, none too happy about the prank messages or unauthorized access to his voicemail, demanded to know who was on the line. "Who is this?" "This is Regis." "No, this is Regis." "No, *this* is Regis." For reasons never officially stated, but probably relating to the friendship between Regis and the head of CBS radio, the segment was never rebroadcast, and no one ever spoke of it again on the show.

The Don and Mike Show was sometimes polarizing, often thought-provoking, but always entertaining. In 2005, when Don's wife was killed in a tragic car accident, the show slowly began to unravel. Three years later, *The Don and Mike Show* became *The Mike O'Meara Show*, as Don left to redefine his life, personally and professionally. Through the turmoil and upheaval, the new show established itself quickly, maintaining the high ratings of *Don and Mike* while finding a voice of its own.

Regardless of its success, and the success of other "guy talk" shows on the station, *The Mike O'Meara Show* would only air on terrestrial radio for one year. Once driven and energized by strong and occasionally controversial personalities, radio was changing. Outrageous radio DJs were only embraced if they adopted a narrow ideology, either about politics or sports. Personality-driven shows were deemed too expensive as radio revenues bottomed out.

In 2008, WJFK "flipped," changing overnight from "hot talk" to sports talk. Most of the shows were dropped, including *The Mike O'Meara Show*. After dedicating nearly 20 years to making WJFK a money making juggernaut, O'Meara only discovered the station

3

flip a week before it occurred. The die had been cast, the decision had been made, but no one wanted to inform the talent.

After feeling the guillotine of unemployment hanging over his head for long enough, O'Meara had finally confronted WJFK program director Chris Kinard. "Just tell me what the real deal is, please. We're big boys here. We can handle it. I've heard that the station is flipping, and it's going to happen in a week's time." The conversation was heated. According to O'Meara, Kinard came clean with four simple words: "It wasn't my decision."

The phone call marked the end of *The Mike O'Meara Show* on WJFK. The hosts never held a face-to-face meeting with Kinard; they had no opportunity for closure. After 17 years, O'Meara and his team were out. Their network show fell out of syndication, and all of the affiliates were offered a new show, free in perpetuity, if they dropped *The Mike O'Meara Show* without the contractually-mandated 30-show notice. If you will permit the dramatic license, it brings to mind the words of the poem "The Hollow Men" by T.S. Eliot:

> In this last of meeting places
> We grope together
> And avoid speech
> Gathered on this beach of the tumid river ...
>
> *This is the way the world ends*
> *This is the way the world ends*
> *This is the way the world ends*
> *Not with a bang but a whimper.*

The Mike O'Meara Show ended not with a bang but with a whimper. However, the most pivotal moments of your life rarely play out as you'd expect. The end of the show on terrestrial radio led to its rebirth as an online podcast, so the "end" is where the story of *The Mike O'Meara Show* truly begins.

2

THE MIKE O'MEARA SHOW: A PRIMER

In case you are not yet a fan of *The Mike O'Meara Show*, you might need a little context to better understand the rest of this book, to literally get on the same page as the fan base. This chapter should provide all the information you need. It describes the content and structure of the show, explains (for those who are wondering) exactly what a podcast is, lists the people who appear as attributed speakers in this book, and presents a timeline of important events for reference.

What is The Mike O'Meara Show?

The Mike O'Meara Show, or *TMOS*, officially describes itself as "a fun mash-up of real life, pop culture, news of the day, dynamic audio clips, and three guys busting each others' balls." If you think that sounds vague, you're right. The show does not anchor itself to a single premise such as politics, sports, pop culture, hard news, or current events. While all of these ingredients work themselves into the mix every week, the proportions of those ingredients change. One thing remains constant: *TMOS* is primarily about the lives of its hosts: Mike O'Meara, Robb Spewak, and Oscar Santana.

Speaking as a longtime fan of *TMOS*, you come for the comedy and stay for the authenticity. On a daily basis, the three men open doors to their lives, sometimes discussing deeply personal issues and other times simply joking around. While they are acutely aware that a large audience is listening in, and they work hard to cater to that audience, they do so effortlessly, like all true broadcast professionals.

Imagine that you've been invited to a party thrown by someone at work—an acquaintance whom you do not know very well. Once you arrive at the party, you wander around looking for someone to talk to, someone to laugh with, someone *interesting*. You round a corner and there are three men holding court. Even though they are already surrounded by a group of people, they see you and wave you over. You may know nothing about them, but they immediately engage you in conversation as if you'd been friends for ages.

They're talking about their relationships, their hopes, their dreams, their frustrations, even their own shortcomings as parents and spouses. Their stories are amazing and engaging no matter what they are talking about. In fact, one of the men has been playfully ranting now for 30 minutes about how much trash he produces in a two-person house. By comparison, his neighbor seems to generate one tiny cube of trash per week and might as well tie it up with a tiny red bow that celebrates his environmental conscientiousness. Those 30 minutes pass like a second, because you find yourself hanging on every word.

That's *TMOS* in a nutshell. These three guys want you to come join the party. They welcome you with open arms, buy you a beer, and then make fun of the way you dress in a good-hearted, offhand manner that instantly endears them to you. You know that you could give it right back to them, and rather than get offended, they'd laugh harder and like you more. *TMOS* is a come-as-you-are, unpretentious show that's open and accessible to all. It's three guys making each other laugh, knowing that all of their listeners are laughing along with them.

Show Content and Structure

Every *TMOS* show begins with a segment known as the "vignette," "show open," or "cold open." The following transcript is the vignette for episode 838, which aired on June 19, 2013. In my opinion, it exhibits all the hallmarks of *TMOS*, so it may help you understand the tone and voice of the show if you have never listened. This show begins with Mike O'Meara declaring that he is frustrated with his dental floss. That simple premise, alone, is enough for Mike, Robb, and Oscar to weave a hilarious and ludicrous tapestry for their listeners.

Transcript of TMOS Episode #838: June 19, 2013 Opening Vignette

Mike O'Meara
A Mike O'Meara investigative report. I've thought about this for a long time, but I have not made it public. The subject today: dental floss. Here's my point. There is a monopoly on dental floss in America. You have two primary companies.

Robb Spewak
Then it's a duopoly.

Mike O'Meara
Alright, a duopoly.

Oscar Santana
Hey! Get it right! Duopoly!

Mike O'Meara
There are two companies that seem to have a corner on the market. There's Reach, and there's Glide ...

Robb Spewak
What about Oral-B?

Mike O'Meara
Aren't they all made by the same people?

Oscar Santana
A triopoly.

Mike O'Meara
Let me look it up here. I'm Googling "dental floss." Let's see what I get. Here we go. Oral-B, Glide, Glide, and then Robb's favorite. You like Plackers, right?

Robb Spewak
Plackers are awesome.

Oscar Santana
Oooooooooooh.

Robb Spewak
Hold it. Was that a "boo" or an "oooh"?

Oscar Santana
"Oooh."

Robb Spewak
Yeah, boy!

Mike O'Meara
I don't like Plackers.

Oscar Santana
Are those the individual picks?

Robb Spewak
It's like a U-shape dealy with two Kevlar strings, and they

really saved my teeth. Do you know that my dentist, *our* dentist, has called my gingiva "dazzling"?

Mike O'Meara
Gingiva?

Robb Spewak
Gingiva.

Oscar Santana
I've had probably four or five deep gum cleaning procedures done in my life, simply because I haven't flossed enough.

Mike O'Meara
Really?

Oscar Santana
I floss now with the little Dentek placards, and I don't ...

Robb Spewak
Plackers.

Mike O'Meara
A "placard" is a sign you would hold up.

Mike O'Meara
So you use the same product that Robb uses?

Oscar Santana
Yes, and we haven't had this conversation.

Robb Spewak
Common ground.

Oscar Santana
My mom uses a sewing kit, though.

Robb Spewak
Like a needle?

Oscar Santana

She uses a needle and thread, or just the thread, like instead of sewing up a dress, she just works those chompers. She's foreign.

Robb Spewak

(laughing)

Mike O'Meara

These are the products I am seeing on the website that you can choose between: Glide, Glide, Glide, Plackers, and I don't know who they're made by.

Oscar Santana

They're certainly not placards.

Mike O'Meara

Product 1: Glide. Product 2: Glide. Product 3: Glide. Product 4: Plackers. Product 5: Glide. And then we get to Reach.

Oscar Santana

What's your beef then?

Mike O'Meara

(Yelling) My beef is I'd like to have some variety in dental floss, because the Glide I am using breaks every time I use it, and I don't have dog teeth. It severs every time, and it's a complete rip-off. It sucks!

Robb Spewak

I was always troubled when I would try to floss with the actual string that it cuts off the circulation in your fingers and you get that big, red fingertip.

Mike O'Meara

I don't care about that because I am a manly man!

Robb Spewak

Yeah, you'll be caring when you stroke out.

Oscar Santana

How do you break plastic? You must be *violent* about it.

Mike O'Meara

No, I just like to get it done.

Robb Spewak

Shards of teeth shooting across the room.

Oscar Santana

(In a tough guy voice) "Carla, I'm gonna go floss."

Mike O'Meara

I like to get deep in there.

Robb Spewak

Yeah you do! No sawing, though.

Mike O'Meara

Well, you're not supposed to saw. You're supposed to go up and down.

Robb Spewak

(Suggestively) Yeah, boy. Yeah, you are!

Oscar Santana

Paint the fence.

Mike O'Meara

(Increasingly agitated) I don't think I'm alone here!

Robb Spewak

I don't know ...

Mike O'Meara

We have a conspiracy, and please open your eyes. Listen to me carefully. I take you to the hypothetical board of directors of the Glide dental floss company.

Robb Spewak

Do they all have mustaches and gray hair?

Mike O'Meara

They're all sitting there like Monopoly men.

Robb Spewak

(Laughing) Top hats?

Mike O'Meara

They all have top hats, ties, and tails.

Oscar Santana

And monocles.

Mike O'Meara

They're sitting there right now. Mr. Burns is at the head of the table and he says, "Why, our sales have stagnated. Why is the company losing money?" And then Smithers is sitting over there in the corner and Smithers says, "Well, it's probably because you make too good a product, sir."

(In Burns' voice) "What if we were to design a floss that broke regularly? Why, they'd throw it out in droves!"

I have a thing of Glide floss up in my bathroom that I just threw away. I opened it up like three days ago because I break so much of the stuff. This is a conspiracy by the dental floss people!

Robb Spewak

This is why Plackers is thinking outside the box, Mike. Their floss is made of Kevlar.

Mike O'Meara

It is not. You're lying. You're not taking me seriously.

Oscar Santana

It's a close cousin of Kevlar, I think.

Robb Spewak

What they do is on the little U-shaped thing, there's two strings, so in the *rare* instance that it breaks, you're still good.

Oscar Santana

You can hang from a building like those Krazy Glue ads from the 80s.

Mike O'Meara

You think it's a better value?

Robb Spewak

I do!

Oscar Santana

Have you thought of yarn?

Robb Spewak

Twine?

Mike O'Meara

See, I hate those things. Sticking a whole piece of plastic in my mouth just to floss. I hate those.

Robb Spewak

It's putting less things in your mouth than before. What if I brought you, tomorrow, a bag of them?

Mike O'Meara

A bag of your used Plackers?

Robb Spewak

No, no. Brand new Plackers because I buy them by the case.

Oscar Santana

What about rope?

Mike O'Meara

Listen, I had floss that was extra strength. Strong but also waxed. I used it and it was amazing! It never broke.

Robb Spewak

You ever use it to tie down a boat? I mean how strong was this?

Mike O'Meara

My floss breaks all the time, and I don't have *shards* of teeth in there. I have wonderful, beautiful, artificial teeth.

Robb Spewak

How about a beaded chain?

Mike O'Meara

How about you take me seriously? The dental floss companies are trying to rip us off and they're trying to take advantage of us. We are going like lambs to the slaughter! See, I am addicted to floss. I floss in the morning and I floss at night.

Robb Spewak

You see, addiction is unhealthy and that's probably why it's breaking.

Mike O'Meara

Forget it. Start the show. ∎

The real meat of the show follows the vignette, based on discussion topics prepared by Mike ahead of time. The final two segments of the show are reserved for regularly recurring features. The penultimate segment of the show is titled "News You May Not Need," and in it Mike presents his take on the news, including many stories that run under the radar of traditional news broadcasts. Oscar fills in for Mike with an entertainment report every Friday. The final segment of each show is the "Audio Vault," in which Robb Spewak hosts a daily smorgasbord of compelling audio clips.

What is a Podcast?

When *TMOS* broadcasted on network radio, based out of WJFK 106.7 FM in Washington, D.C., the show ran for four hours a day during afternoon drive time, from 3 p.m. to 7 p.m. In the newest incarnation of the program—the podcast—each show is exactly 79 minutes long. As you will learn later in the book (if you do not already know), these podcasts are recorded and produced in Mike O'Meara's living room.

You can find *TMOS* on the air in Iowa, on radio station KCJJ 1630 AM. Adding commercials expands the show to two hours, which is why *TMOS* maintains a 79-minute running time. It is broadcast-ready and Federal Communication Commission (FCC) compliant. What do radio stations need to do in order to run *TMOS* on the air? Just insert ads.

However, until more affiliates broadcast the show on terrestrial radio, those of us who do not live in Iowa access the show via the podcast. A podcast is nothing more than a series of audio files, usually MP3 files, which is the same file format as most digital music. Using a variety of software applications, including iTunes, you can search for and subscribe to most podcasts (including *TMOS*) for free with a click of a button. Once you subscribe, all future episodes of the podcast are automatically delivered to your computer, smart phone, or MP3 player.

In this way, podcasts are for audio content what digital video recorders (DVRs, including brands such as TiVo) are for television. You can listen to any downloaded show at any time; it's radio on demand. While the portable nature of podcasts makes them truly versatile, you do not need an MP3 player or a smart phone to listen. Visit *www.mikeomearashow.com*, and you'll find all of the most recent episodes right there on the front page of the website. Click the "play" button and enjoy your transformation into a *TMOS* fan. You're welcome in advance.

Collaborator Biographies

The following people are quoted in this book; they are listed alphabetically by first name. Many of them graciously donated their time, speaking with me at length on the phone. Without their cooperation, this book would not have been possible.

Arch Campbell: A 40-year veteran television broadcaster in the Washington, D.C. region who has reported entertainment news for WRC-TV NBC Channel 4 and WJLA ABC Channel 7 and also hosts a weekly television show on the regional cable network NewsChannel 8

Buzz Burbank: Former newsman of *The Don and Mike Show* and *The Mike O'Meara Show*

Carla O'Meara: Wife of Mike O'Meara, co-owner of a court reporting company, and first-time mom to baby boy Michael William O'Meara in 2013

Catherine O'Meara: Elder daughter of Mike O'Meara's three children, a college freshman in 2013

Cathy Parshley: (née Cathy O'Meara) Older sister and only sibling of Mike O'Meara

Elizabeth O'Meara: Younger daughter of Mike O'Meara, a high school junior in 2013

Kappy Pfeiffer: Friend of *TMOS* whose generosity helped establish the podcast and after whom the broadcast studio ("The Kappy Pfeiffer Studio") is named

Mary O'Meara: Mother of Mike O'Meara and Cathy Parshley

Mike O'Meara: The titular host of *The Mike O'Meara Show*, a self-proclaimed Irish storyteller in his mid-50s, former restaurateur, Harley Davidson enthusiast, and a new dad in 2013

Oscar Santana: Cohost of *The Mike O'Meara Show* who joined the team when his show, *The Big O and Dukes Show*, was also cancelled as a result of the WJFK format change

Robb Spewak: Cohost of *The Mike O'Meara Show*, formerly an intern and producer of *The Don and Mike Show*, who manages the audio for the show and loves to harass telemarketers

Steve Bridges: Owner of "The Mighty 1630 KCJJ" radio station in Coralville, Iowa, the network affiliate of *The Mike O'Meara Show* podcast and affiliate of *The Mike O'Meara Show* during its run on terrestrial radio

Tony Perkins: Current evening news anchorman at WTTG FOX Channel 5 in Washington, D.C., weatherman for *Good Morning America* from 1999 to 2005, and former classmate of Mike O'Meara at American University

Timeline of Important Events

June 22, 1959: Mike O'Meara is born

1981: Mike O'Meara graduates from American University

1985: Mike O'Meara first partners with Don Geronimo

1985–1991: Mike O'Meara cohosts the *Morning Zoo* and *The Don and Mike Show* with Don Geronimo on WAVA 105.1 FM in Washington, D.C.

1991–2008: Mike O'Meara cohosts *The Don and Mike Show* with Don Geronimo on WJFK 106.7 FM in Washington, D.C.

April 14, 2008: *The Don and Mike Show* becomes *The Mike O'Meara Show* on WJFK when Geronimo leaves the broadcast

July 17, 2009: The final episode of the four-hour terrestrial radio incarnation of *The Mike O'Meara Show* airs

July 20, 2009: WJFK flips formats to sports talk

September 12, 2009: Mike O'Meara weds Carla O'Meara (née Rackovan)

December 7, 2009: The first episode of *The Mike O'Meara Show* podcast airs

July 7, 2010: *The Kirk and Mike Show* begins, featuring Kirk McEwen and Mike O'Meara, on classic rock radio station WVRX 105.9 FM "The Edge" in Washington, D.C.

September 19, 2011: *The Kirk and Mike Show* ends as WVRX no longer broadcasts original content but instead simulcasts conservative news station WMAL 630 AM

March 31, 2012: The State Theater in Falls Church, Virginia, hosts the first live *Mike O'Meara Show*

February 19, 2014: The 1,000th regular episode of *The Mike O'Meara Show* podcast airs (excluding bonus shows, live shows, and premium content)

3

O'MEARICAN HISTORY

If you were to analyze the most successful books and films in history, you might be surprised to find that their stories have the same universal structure, in the same sequence. (1) A hero arises with a specific need. (2) The hero battles an enemy to meet that need. (3) The hero defeats the enemy by making a critical, life-changing choice. (4) The hero is fundamentally changed by the battle, usually for the better.

Almost every good story follows this model regardless of its tone or genre:

- Dorothy in *The Wizard of Oz* needs to get home, so she teams up with an unlikely group to defeat a wicked witch.

- Andy Dufresne in *The Shawshank Redemption* fights for freedom from wrongful imprisonment and a twisted prison warden.

- George Bailey in *It's a Wonderful Life* seeks purpose as he fights internal and external forces in the form of suicidal depression and a wheelchair-bound banker, respectively.

- In *Transformers 2*, one kind of robot has to fight another kind of robot because of some sort of robot thing, which is somehow resolved by Megan Fox running in slow motion while wearing a tank top.

The *TMOS* story, the major narrative of this book, is also a simple story at heart: a group of radio personalities seeks a new way to broadcast after being unceremoniously kicked off the air.

If most stories have the same structure, why do they feel so unique? The characters. Once you can relate to the characters, when you can see the story through their eyes and from their perspectives, only then does the story truly come to life. Therefore, in Chapters 3 and 4 we explore the main characters of this story, beginning with the man whose name adorns the show.

Origin Story

Mike O'Meara
I was born in Hartford Hospital on June 22, 1959, the son of Mary and Bill O'Meara of Glastonbury, Connecticut.

Cathy Parshley
Mike was born early because he was sort of small, ironically. Go figure that. He was a little, tiny baby, around 5 or 6 pounds. He had some breathing problems at birth, so he stayed at the hospital for a few extra days.

Mike O'Meara
The performer in me comes from my mom, and so does the gregarious person in me. She is very outgoing and a lot of fun to be around.

Mary O'Meara

Mike makes friends easily. I think he likes people. Even though that doesn't come out all of the time on his show, I think he likes people.

Mike O'Meara

William Joseph O'Meara, my father, was a World War II veteran, a captain in the United States Army. He lost his mother, I think, when he was six years old. She had a strep infection, and that killed you in those days. He lost his father in his mid-teens. He was raised by his mother's sisters, who were these old Irish aunts that I grew up visiting. I think because my parents both had a lot of loss early in their lives, that might have helped bring them together.

When I was nine, I remember my mom saying something like, "I love you more than you will ever know, but your father will always come first." I don't know if that's the direct quote, but I know that she made it very clear. Although she loved me, her relationship with my father was a true love story.

Mary O'Meara

Bill was the oldest father on the street and yet he would get out and play with the kids. He'd go out to the ball field and shag balls, where the other fathers weren't doing it even though they were quite a bit younger—maybe five or six years younger than he was.

Cathy Parshley

One of my mother's favorite stories involves my father going to the nursery at the hospital and peering through the window at the new babies in the newborn area. Someone came up behind him and asked him if this was his first grandchild, to which he responded with great indignation, "No, it's my son, my first son."

Mike O'Meara

I will always remember my father, especially as he got older, sitting in that corner chair in the living room. I would be able to tell by the position of the drink in his hand whether the Red Sox were winning or losing that night. If I came home and his glass was sitting straight up on the table, then it was a nail-biter, a close game. If he was holding the glass and it was kind of leaning forward, then I would know that the Red Sox were getting their butts kicked. If he was just sitting there with the glass in his hands, they were probably losing, but they were still in it.

Mike Kelley

You didn't mention any posture for your father that indicated the Red Sox were winning.

Mike O'Meara

Correct. Red Sox fans are kind of fatalistic. We focus on the negative.

Sibling Rivalry

Mary O'Meara

My two children, Mike and Cathy, were born so many years apart that even though they loved each other, there were some sore points. Cathy liked to boss Mike around and Mike didn't like that very much.

Mike O'Meara

It's difficult to relate to someone who is that much older than you are.

Cathy Parshley

The age difference is almost seven years, so it's significant. When Mike was born, I was in first grade. I really wanted a sibling, and my parents hoped to have several in between the two of us, which didn't quite work out for them. We came from a Catholic family, and my mother's wish was to fill up a pew at church on Sunday. The reality didn't live up to that expectation.

I was very protective of Mike, being much older. He was the younger child and he played on my mother's sympathies a lot. My mother to this day will admit that she somewhat coddled him. My role was to toughen him up a bit. He'll be the first to tell you that.

Mike O'Meara

When I was a kid, my sister loved to torture me. When I was five or six years old, we went to the Grange Fair in Glastonbury, Connecticut. I was always very excited to go, because back in those days, we didn't have the kind of amusement parks you have now. When the fair came to town, it was a really big deal. Cathy and I went down to the fair, and there was a ride called the Octopus.

Cathy Parshley

The Octopus was really the only scary ride. He was kind of eyeing it, and I was caring for him that day, kind of walking him around, as I often did.

Mike O'Meara

All I know is that my sister and I stood in line, and she said, "It's not scary. You are going to be fine."

Cathy Parshley

I coaxed him onto the ride saying, "It doesn't go fast. It's really not scary, it's fun. Come on, don't be a wimp. Do it!"

Mike O'Meara

I was nervous because I was hearing the kids scream as they rode it. When we finally got into the ride, and they put us both in the bucket and closed the door ...

Cathy Parshley

I turned to him and I said, "By the way, it goes REALLY fast, and it's REALLY scary!"

Mike O'Meara

When it started to move, I started screaming.

Cathy Parshley

He freaked out.

Mike O'Meara

I screamed so loudly that they had to stop the ride and let me out of the Octopus. That was my first memory of my sister torturing me.

Cathy Parshley

No, no. They didn't stop the ride. He sniffled and cried, but he got through it, and he was all the better for it. So that's one example where I definitely fulfilled my role as an older sister, giving him a reality check and toughening him up a bit.

Mike O'Meara

That's what a seven year age difference will do for you. No remorse! Then there's the most famous story about my sister Cathy, where I was playing hockey on the pond all day. We would play from the early morning until dark.

Cathy Parshley

We had a pond behind our house that was a kids' paradise growing up.

Mike O'Meara

Unfortunately, late in the day, I was so absorbed in the hockey game that I ignored the fecal urgency that had been building all day long. I had to go! I had to go badly.

Cathy Parshley

I was much older then. I was probably 15 and he was, what, 9 or 10?

Mike O'Meara

I ran up the short hill to our house with my skates on. We would wear the skates through the leaves and snow, so it wouldn't really hurt the skates that much. When I got home, I would normally take my skates off. Well, I got to the door and I said, "Cathy, I need to use the bathroom and I don't have time to take my skates off."

Cathy Parshley

I wouldn't let him in with his hockey gear on.

Mike O'Meara

She said, "No, you can't wear your skates in the house." I said, "I have to go bad! I gotta go poo!" And she said, "No, you can't...." I crapped my pants.

Cathy Parshley

And *of course*, when my parents got home, I was the one who got in trouble for that. I *humiliated* him and he does love to tell that story.

Mike O'Meara

I guess this was another time she was trying to "toughen me up," by strengthening my bowels.

Cathy Parshley

He doesn't talk about me having to help him clean that up while mumbling curses under my breath.

———

Mary O'Meara

After Cathy graduated from college, she tried to tell me how to raise Mike.

Cathy Parshley

That first year out of college I worked in inner-city Hartford as a first-year teacher, because that was the only job I could get. I lived back home with Mike and my parents for a year. My brother was ruthless when I moved back home, very brutal to me saying, "Why are you here? Aren't you supposed to be living somewhere else at this point?" I always weighed in whenever there was a concern about his behavior or his academics. I don't think he appreciated that.

Even though I felt it was my role to toughen him up and show him the real world, there was a flip side. I was also very protective of him and looked out for him. I remember taking care of him during his first drunken state. It was when I had moved back home to my parents' house. I was probably 21, which made him 15.

Mike O'Meara

I went up to my friend Joey's house and some girls from the neighborhood snuck into their fathers' liquor cabinets.

Cathy Parshley

Of course, it's always the girls who get blamed. They mixed some concoction together, all the alcohol they could find and probably some Hawaiian Punch to sweeten the pot.

Mike O'Meara

I drank a lot of it and got as sick as a dog. I dragged my sleeping bag all the way home overnight and scratched on my sister's window so she'd let me in.

Cathy Parshley

At that time I was living in the bottom level of my family's house, and I heard this scratching on my window screen. I was like, "Oh my God, oh my God. He's been sick all night and he just walked all the way from Apple Hill," which was about three miles away, "and I think he's going to pass out."

Mike O'Meara

Cathy cried because I looked so pathetic. I'd thrown up. I think I might have pooped on the lawn at Joey's house. Why do all of these stories involve me defecating?

Cathy Parshley

My mother came downstairs, whisked open the window, and said, "He's not sick! He's *drunk*!" That was a situation where the tables turned. My mother was completely unsympathetic and I was nice to Mike.

———

Mike O'Meara

My family can be ruthless with its comedy, but as a group we are hysterically funny. Here's the perfect example, the story I like to tell about our family's sense of humor. We're together in a car, Carla, my daughters Catherine and Elizabeth, my sister, and my mother. We were all in Massachusetts, right outside of Boston, to see the facility where my mom was going to be moving to. It was a difficult weekend for me, very emotional, because it's hard to see a parent go into any kind of home that has nursing facilities attached to it. At the same time, we knew it was a nice place and we knew my mom was going to be happy there, but it was still kind of a sad weekend.

We're driving, and my sister's describing the assisted living community that my mom's moving to.

Mary O'Meara

When Mike first came up, he hadn't seen the facility, so Cathy was explaining everything to him. She was saying, "Now in Phase One, Mom's going to be completely independent in her apartment."

29

Mike O'Meara

"In Phase One, you get to come and go as you please. If you want to have a car, you can have a car. You can get the meals they have at the facility, you can go out to eat, or you can make your own meals. You basically do whatever you want."

Mary O'Meara

"And if Mom needs help, she can go to Phase Two, which is assisted living where she will still have some independence."

Mike O'Meara

"Phase Three is, of course, the full nursing home that's on the grounds, if she needs full-time care." At the moment Cathy is discussing Phase Three, and this is a true story, the car is driving by a cemetery. Without missing a beat, Cathy points out the window and says, "If you look to your left, that would be Phase Four."

The whole car, we all cracked up, because that is the way our family is. Right after that, when we saw the cemetery, I think there was an ambulance that came by, and Cathy said, "Hey, Mom, I think one of the rooms just opened up for you." It was bittersweet, but it's the way we handle stuff. We've always been able to laugh in my family.

Mary O'Meara

The whole family has a good sense of humor. I always say we are a little bit crazy, but better to laugh than to cry.

Molding a Broadcaster

Mike O'Meara

The singular experiences that molded me into a radio person happened in my house in Maine, a group house owned by a million different family members. Back in the day we had all the kids running around, my father, his brother, and his sister.

After dinner, they would retire to the living room, where on any given night during the summer there would be a spirited discussion of the issues of the day, local events, national politics, anything. My father was a moderate Democrat. My Aunt Mary, his sister, was a Vassar-educated liberal Democrat. My Uncle Ted was a very staunch Republican.

They would debate, all very bright and well-educated people who were different politically. There would be times when I was halfway up the street and I could still hear the "discussions" going on. They loved to give their opinions. They loved to argue. As kids, we had to function in that environment. You were encouraged to be articulate. You were encouraged to give your opinions and listen to people who were skilled at expressing themselves—almost to a fault. I grew up in a very verbal environment.

I used to be fascinated by their discussions. I would come home from playing with my friends, walk into the living room, and just watch and listen to them. It was always fascinating to me because they were all very strong personalities. They'd have some wonderful discussions. Being in that environment, it rubs off on you.

My father was another influence on my career. He was an audiophile. We had a very small den, and in a closet off of the den, on a couple of shelves, he had a turntable and an amplifier. There were speakers in the den, and my dad also ran speakers out into the living room. When I think back to it, it makes me emotional. That hi-fi system was the centerpiece of the house.

Mary O'Meara

Bill bought Mike a remote microphone for the hi-fi. He was probably only about 12 or 13, around that age. He would do broadcasts over the hi-fi that you could hear throughout the house.

Mike O'Meara

I probably drove them nuts doing it, because I was in love with the microphone at a very, very young age. The microphone itself represents a lot to people in the radio business. You are fascinated by the idea of amplifying your own voice. It's intoxicating. When I heard my voice coming through those speakers, that's when everything started.

Mary O'Meara

Mike could impersonate so many voices, even as a youngster. I remember once he did the Indianapolis 500. He would make the sounds of the motors, do the commentary, the commercials, segues, everything. Even way back I just knew he was going to do something in broadcasting.

Mike O'Meara

The layout of our tiny little den, where we had that stereo system, was interesting. We had a center hallway cape, so the way our house was situated, the den was on the right side of the house. There was this little section of the hallway that opened into the den. I always thought of it as a stage. I would perform in front of my folks. That was my little theatrical area, the "performance center" of the house.

Cathy Parshley

Put a microphone in his hand, and Mike would sing. I remember him with the wireless microphone, going upstairs and getting some clothing from my mother's bedroom, including ... well, let's just say he had no problem dressing in drag. I bet people don't know that about him.

He would put on some flowing garb with this huge straw hat and he'd come swooping down the stairway with his wireless mic, belting out, "The hills are alive with the sound of music!" He was always doing things like that as a kid.

Mike O'Meara

That might have been around the time of the Glastonbury High School "Non-Talent Talent Show," which we had every year. I think I opened the show one year. I test-drove my act for Cathy and her friends, who were over one night, by playing the title song from *The Sound of Music,* sung by Julie Andrews, and singing along.

It was performed absolutely exquisitely by yours truly, wearing one of my mother's dresses and one of her large, floppy summer hats. I performed it on the stage of Glastonbury High School, but first I did a private show for my sister and her friends.

It wasn't the first or the last time that I would be in drag. I've gone to parties dressed as Barbara Bush. I'm comfortable in pumps, and I'm comfortable in a dress—as comfortable as any man of my size can be.

Cathy Parshley

Isn't it ironic? He's back home with his wireless mic. Probably still dressing in drag, but he doesn't let you know that.

Mike O'Meara

I started my career by doing a show in my living room and here I am again, doing another show in my living room. It just keeps getting better—that's what I love about doing this. The thing is, though, when I pull the curtain closed in this living room studio to start the podcast, this is no longer my home.

I don't even think of it in those terms; I think about the broadcast. I could be in any studio, and I could do this show in any room in the world. Is it cool to do the show from my house? Yeah, it's terrific. I love it. I can understand why a lot of other broadcasters have done this, setting up studios in their homes. Put a microphone in front of me, plug it into something, send out a signal over the Internet or over the air, and I'll do it.

———

Mike O'Meara

After high school, I went to Marist College in Poughkeepsie, New York. It's where Bill O'Reilly attended college, on the banks of the Hudson River in scenic, beautiful Poughkeepsie. It's the "other school" in Poughkeepsie. There's another little school just up the road a piece called Vassar, where people with decent GPAs went.

I transferred from Marist to American University in Washington, D.C. in 1979. I transferred because I was not happy at Marist. I didn't feel a connection with the student body. Even though I enjoyed the theater program, I wanted bigger, a little better, a city school.

American University was where I wanted to be. I also transferred because I did not care for New York all that much. It seemed like everyone there came from Long Island and had big, heavy Yankee fan accents. There were just too many goddamned Yankee fans at that school. I started my junior year at American University, and that's when I met Tony Perkins.

Tony Perkins

At American University, we had a bar/restaurant in one of the main buildings on campus called the Tavern. It was where everybody hung out. Mike would be there quite a bit.

I believe Mike would DJ there sometimes. Because I was on the radio, and because I was a funny guy, I would emcee shows there—I enjoyed doing standup comedy.

One of my earliest memories of Mike is at one of my emcee jobs, laughing and really encouraging me. Mike and I ran across each other quite a bit in college, often at the radio station. We were friends—not the best of friends. I wasn't one of his "hangin' buddies," and he wasn't one of mine, but we were friends. We lost touch with each other pretty quickly after college. Remember, this is in the days before Facebook and all that kind of stuff, but that was short-lived.

Mike O'Meara

I hired Tony as a disc jockey on WYRE 810 AM in Annapolis when I was the program director there.

Tony Perkins

I started doing stand-up comedy again when I was working in Annapolis. Mike would come see me perform. We started to get a little closer during that time. He thought I was funny, and he was very encouraging. He'd come see me and laugh.

Mike O'Meara

Over the years—it's funny—I have seen Tony infrequently, but we have always managed to maintain a friendship and keep in sporadic contact. Usually it's in a professional context, where I'll see him on his TV set or he'll come by and panel on my radio show. I think we've maintained contact over the years because we've both been working in broadcasting— Tony in television and me doing this clown college thing that I have here.

Tony Perkins

My friendship with Mike is the most unusual relationship I have, because while I am a friend of his, I am also a bona fide fan. I am *such* a fan.

One day a couple of years ago, when Mike was doing his own show at WJFK, he had some medical procedure—surgery or something. They called and asked if I would come and fill in for him one day. One of the highlights of my career! Honestly, I am not making this up. It was spectacular, just to be in that world for four full hours.

As much as I have enjoyed everything I have done, I don't have the freedom that Mike has had on his radio shows. I am given a lot of leeway on my Channel 5 show, but in Mike's job, every day, you can pretty much do and say whatever you want. For someone like me, that is a *dream*. That's a dream.

Modern Family

Carla O'Meara

One night after work, my business partners, Joey and Jerry, and I went out to have a drink together. We own a court reporting company. At that point in my life, I was smoking, and I would stick my ID—my driver's license—in the cellophane of the cigarette pack. That night I finished the pack and threw it away with my ID inside.

Joey and Jerry still wanted to go out, but because I didn't have my ID, I had to go to the one bar where the owners knew I was old enough to drink. I had just turned 23, so I was young and I looked it. Mike was at the bar.

After the bar closed, Jerry said, "Let's have people come back to the house," his house, and Mike happened to be one of them. I remember sitting inside and Mike was sitting outside. We caught each other's eye a couple of times.

Mike O'Meara

I knew early on by looking at her that I had a few years on her. I remember sitting with a friend of mine on this patio, and she was sitting inside in the kitchen. All these 20-something guys were doing fly-bys. She wasn't paying much attention to them, and I watched this with a great deal of amusement. I was pleased. She wasn't giving those guys the time of day, so I took a chance and talked to her.

Carla O'Meara

Once we started talking, we never stopped talking.

Cathy Parshley

The family certainly raised its eyebrows when Mike began to get serious with someone who is a year younger than my daughter. She is a generation younger than he is.

Carla O'Meara

Mike had just turned 43; I had just turned 23.

Cathy Parshley

I guess looking from the outside, we all thought, "Oh, come on. What are you doing? What's this all about? Are you kidding me?" Truthfully, I don't think any of us expected it to last. He didn't have a great track record with marriage, so I think we were all skeptical about him going into another relationship.

Mike O'Meara

Carla takes me for me. She knows who I am. God, she knows me well. She lets me be me, and I do the same thing with her. That's really the key to success. When you try to change somebody or you're not happy with somebody and you can't accept their shortcomings in any way, you're screwed.

Cathy Parshley

When Mike first started dating her, he said, "There are two things I can promise you: you will never meet her and Mom will never meet her."

As their relationship got more serious, it became obvious that, of course, we were going to have her in our lives, too. We all love her, and she's done a lot for Mike.

Mike O'Meara

Now that I am as old as I am, I have learned how important your immediate family is, how that's ultimately what life is all about. Now, other people's successes bring me more joy than my own. When I see that my kids are doing well, like my daughter getting early admission into Mary Washington University, that was one of the best days of my life. I felt so wonderful for her, so happy for her.

I think that's real success in life. I've had some bumps in the road. I've been married three times. Now, getting through all that, coming out on the other side, I have loving relationships with my daughters and I'm married to a woman whom I love very much. I couldn't be more content, more satisfied.

Getting through those bumps, however, meant I had to take the high road more than once in my life. I had to choose not to go to war for a short-term feeling of satisfaction, revenge, or some sense of justice. When you take the high road, you emerge a happier person. Especially when people go through a divorce, they want to lash out, they want to punish, they want to hurt, but that doesn't do anyone any good.

Elizabeth O'Meara

I was really young when the divorce happened.

Catherine O'Meara

I was 6 and Elizabeth was 4. I was in first grade.

Mike O'Meara

I've told friends of mine who were going through divorces that even though they may want to fight a War of the Roses at that moment, at the end of the day it won't do them any good, especially if there are kids involved. I really believe that with all of my heart.

When I see my kids, they still hug me and love me. In my opinion, that is a great accomplishment, because that's not how all divorces end. I worked very hard and had a lot of pain in my life going through my divorces, but I have always tried to take the high road whenever I could.

———

Carla O'Meara
I'm not just saying this, but Mike's daughters, Catherine and Elizabeth, have been really, really good kids as long as I have known them. I think you can do your best to try and raise your kids well, but ultimately they are who they are. Either they are good or they are not so good. Mike is really blessed to have two really, really good girls. If our son is half as good as they are, I'll be very happy.

Catherine O'Meara
If I had to describe my dad in three words, I would pick passionate, hilarious, and sensitive. He's very sensitive, and not a lot of people know it. He's your typical Irishman.

Elizabeth O'Meara
He cried at the movie *Dolphin's Tale*. He couldn't stop crying for the whole movie.

Catherine O'Meara
He tried to play it off, but we knew what was going on. He can be tough. He can seem like a very tough guy, but he's very sweet underneath it all. Especially to mammals.

Elizabeth O'Meara
We've known Carla since we were 5 and 7, so we've known her most of our lives. We've always liked her.

Carla O'Meara

From the beginning I've always told Mike that I wanted to get married and have kids. At one point about six years into the relationship, I said, "Mike, you know this isn't fair to me or to you. If you want to be with me, and you can't give me what I need in this relationship, please don't keep me. I do want to be with you, but please let me go if you don't want to marry me and have kids."

Mike O'Meara

I was pretty sure I didn't want to have a third child. I just didn't want to start over again. At my age, you kind of feel like you are at the finish line.

Carla O'Meara

We decided to take a break from our relationship, and it lasted about three months. You know the saying, "If you love something, set it free"? We did.

Mike O'Meara

I think every couple should take that kind of break, to see if they really want to be together. Once you spend some time apart, that usually seals the deal. But then who am I to give relationship advice? I've been married three times. However, I'm reasonably confident this one's going to last.

Carla O'Meara

Shortly after, we were back together again, stronger than ever. Ironically, if we hadn't had that break, I don't think we would have stayed together. He wanted to be with me and, ultimately, he agreed to have kids. Now there's a baby on the way.

There are two reasons I think I got pregnant when I did. First of all I read the book *Fifty Shades of Gray*. Second was our trip to Haiti. Mike did a lot of auctions for a charity called

Helping Haitian Angels, a charity for Haitian orphans, so we traveled to Haiti to visit them, to help out.

We got back from Haiti and about a week later, I was talking to Mike about these two little girls I connected with in Haiti, Jennifer and Darlene. I really wanted to adopt both of them. I told Mike I wanted to have kids, so it was either have a kid of our own or adopt these two girls.

We talked about it. Mike knew that I was serious about it, but before we could work on the logistics, I found out I was pregnant. That ended the adoption discussion fairly quickly. I don't think either of us was ready for three new kids at once.

Catherine O'Meara

I remember Elizabeth being really little, probably about 4 or 5, and every single Christmas for a few years, she would always ask for a baby brother for Christmas. So, she got her Christmas wish; it just took a few years.

Mike O'Meara

My family keeps me grounded, they keep me going. There's nothing more important, and as much as I love my work, if I ever had to make a choice, I'd choose family first. As I've gotten older, I've realized that the only source of true happiness is making other people in your life happy.

You can do a lot of things for yourself—you can make a lot of money and you can buy a lot of nice things. That won't, ultimately, make you happy. The happiest moments of my life are when I am in a car, a restaurant, my home, anywhere, with my wife and daughters. If they're giving me a lot of crap, because I'm the "stupid dad," then I'm even happier. If you want to narrowcast a little bit more, then I'd be even happier if this was all happening at the movies. Carla's not a big movie buff, so we don't go together very often.

If I can get Carla to come out to the movies with both of my daughters, if it's me, Carla, Catherine, and Elizabeth side-by-side in a movie theater, that's all I need. That's about it. You're looking at the happiest man in the world, before the movie starts that is, because if it's a shitty movie, then all bets are off.

Now that I have a young son on the way, one of my main life goals is not to die soon. I really would like to try to stay alive. When you're an older father, that's your primary objective. You want to be around. You want to enjoy the good times and be a positive influence on your child's life. This is going to be my first son, and I want to see and do all of the things that dads do with sons. I think about that more than anything else. I want to be sharp, not a doddering old fool when he's in high school. I'm hoping that modern medicine will help me accomplish that.

———

Carla O'Meara

What drives me crazy about Mike? If he ain't bitchin', he ain't breathin'. If I had a magic wand and could change something about Mike, no doubt about it, I'd choose his bitching, especially when he's driving. "Oh, that person's texting," "That person's fed up because he saw I wanted to get over," or "The speed limit is 55, why are they going 30?" It's always something. I mean, oh God, just shut up.

Mike O'Meara

In this Northern Virginia corridor, you live in a den of wolves. You let people go ahead of you in traffic and they pull out in front of you as though there was some edict that came down from on high. They command you to move out of their way, and they refuse to acknowledge that you exist.

That said, I wish I wouldn't complain as much as I do. I would change that about myself if I could, but it's almost impossible. I get so ramped up sometimes, it just kills me.

Cathy Parshley

Other than his physical fitness, what drives me crazy about Mike? I honestly can't think of one thing. If you would have asked me that question five years ago I might have said I thought he was the biggest egomaniac.

When he was in his 20s and 30s, he was sort of dismissive toward family. He would get impatient with us. At one point he said, "My fans don't treat me this way." He felt like we should grant him unconditional respect because he was such a star. No matter how famous you get, though, it doesn't make a difference with family. Family always treats you the same. He's not like that anymore, though. He's improved with age.

Mike O'Meara

My biggest fear used to be losing everything—watching it all go away. Having the show go away, having the money go away, losing my job. Most people in radio live in a state of perpetual fear for their gigs, even when they have a guaranteed contract.

I think my biggest fear now is that I will continue to be sharp, that I will keep my edge and continue to get the joke. As I go through my 50s and into my 60s, I still want to understand what's funny. I don't want to evolve into an old fart.

.

4
The Sidekick and the New Guy

The two cohosts of *The Mike O'Meara Show* have precisely one thing in common: they both love broadcasting. Other than that, Robb Spewak and Oscar Santana are, metaphorically, red and violet light—opposite ends of the personality spectrum. Robb is a family man who embraces the suburban life. He maintains annual memberships at the local amusement park and at the local Costco, and he'd consider spending time at either place "a pretty nice little Saturday."

Oscar, on the other hand, is not yet 40, not yet married, and not yet ready to commit to caring for a kitten. He is occasionally looking for true love, often looking for "the next big business opportunity," and always striving to "keep it tight," to maintain his slim frame almost to spite Robb and Mike, who have historically struggled with weight.

In this chapter, we take a moment with the cohosts of *TMOS*, former WJFK employees who cast their lot with Mike O'Meara to resurrect themselves outside the confines of terrestrial radio.

Your Old Buddy, Robb

Robb Spewak has always loved radio. Growing up, he was a huge fan of *The Don and Mike Show*. He was, in fact, one of the regular callers. Every holiday season, starting in high school, Robb would call the show impersonating Jimmy Stewart from *It's a Wonderful Life*, shouting "Merry Christmas, you wonderful old Building and Loan!" He doggedly pursued a radio career through college and eventually landed an internship with Don and Mike. He spent a long time working for that show, and when the opportunity arose to cohost on *The Mike O'Meara Show,* his radio dream had come true.

Unfortunately, radio was dying, so he only enjoyed one year as a cohost before *TMOS* was cancelled. This is well-trod ground for Robb; many of the things he loves (including Elvis, jukeboxes, and black and white films) are fading from modern pop culture. However, in every one of his full-time jobs, throughout his entire adult life, he has worked with Mike O'Meara in broadcasting. He's not about to give up on radio now.

Robb Spewak

My first job was in gardening. I worked at a vegetable stand, starting at age 6 or 7. I was a kid selling vegetables, and that's when I learned how to calculate sales tax in my head. At around 16, I took a job with my grandfather as a furniture store delivery man in Falls Church, Virginia. After a little while lugging furniture around, I learned very quickly that I did not wish to hold a job requiring that sort of exertion. It made radio look really good.

Fast forward to college, at Virginia Commonwealth University, when I worked as a grocery store checker for Safeway in Loudon County, Virginia. I also worked for one of the Safeway stores on campus. I worked all weekend, every weekend. When most kids were out partying or blowing off steam, I was manning a check stand and stocking the dairy case. Work filled every weekend, and it prevented me from having any fun. Ever.

The summer before my senior year in college was a different story. That was the first year of college that I didn't work at a grocery store. Instead, I interned for *The Don and Mike Show*. When my internship was over and I went back to school, that was horrible. I had figured out what I wanted to do with the rest of my life, and now I had to wait out two semesters of college to get to do what I was itching to do.

The Don and Mike Show and the radio station were not union shops. Truth be told, the radio station was barely functional. For me as a tenacious intern, it meant I could learn to do anything. They were happy because they didn't have to pay me. I learned, over the course of time, to run the shows—how to run board, do production. Never getting paid, but having a blast. It was a radio nerd's playground.

After graduation, I asked if I could come and hang out at the station, and they let me back in on a technicality. They classified me as an "unpaid intern." I wasn't really allowed to be there, but I was pretty good at staying under the radar. I was determined that I would get a job there, and I felt like I needed to be there as often as I could, waiting for my opportunity to arise. Luckily, they didn't run the books on me or anything, or they'd have realized I was a squatter. A few months later, I was legitimately hired as a part-timer.

Mike Kelley
Do you all feel like you have achieved what you want to achieve in radio, in broadcasting?

Mike O'Meara
I'll answer that one first. I'm doing a show from my goddamned living room, so the answer would be no.

Robb Spewak

I got into radio largely because of *The Don and Mike Show*. When I was invited by Mike to cohost with him on WJFK, one of my favorite radio stations of all time, it was a tremendous moment for me.

Mike O'Meara

I can actually give you Robb's career timeline. He started as a listener, then became a stalker, then intern, production assistant, producer, production assistant, producer, production assistant, producer, production assistant, cohost, fired.

Oscar Santana

It's like the evolution drawing except it keeps going up and down, back from man to monkey to man to monkey to man and then just a little gravestone.

Robb Spewak

Starting on *The Mike O'Meara Show* was the mountaintop for me. Since then, I see a greater future for all of us on the show, so I would say yes, I am unfulfilled, but I am also eager for the future.

———

Mike O'Meara

What drives me crazy about Robb?

Oscar Santana

There are so many things I hate about Robb. We could start with his fashion sense. He dresses like he's stuck in the 1980s; he's Biff Tannen in *Back to the Future 2*. But picking on Robb's clothes is too easy. What really drives me up the wall is something I actually admire about him, a trait I wish I had: Robb is oblivious. I could walk in tomorrow and tell Robb my car just got repossessed and he'd say, "At least you don't have to pay more bills."

He is Mr. Silver Lining—there's always an upside. I think most people know there's not always an upside in life. Sometimes all of the sides just suck, but not for Robb. The movie *Silver Linings Playbook* should have been about him, minus the mental breakdowns and the jogging and all the ballroom dancing. He's not doing any of that because he hates physical activity. Maybe it's not a great analogy after all.

Mike O'Meara

Robb walks into my kitchen every single day and we have a moment. We might say something funny to one another or recount something that's happened to us; it's a joy. He's a wonderful human being to work with on a daily basis. I love the guy, absolutely.

However, Robb lives in a land of candy canes and puppy dog tails where life is just wonderful. Robb's Pollyanna, "everything's fine, la, la, la" attitude drives me absolutely insane. Robb doesn't seem to be bothered by any of life's issues. It's one of his strengths, but that strength drives me out of my mind. Robb never seems to let anything get to him and I let everything get to me.

Robb Spewak

One of the driving forces that made me want to go into radio was that for my entire life, I have annoyed, interrupted, pissed people off, and cracked jokes at inappropriate times. This got me in all kinds of trouble in school and made me one of the least popular people in my family, but I realized that I could use these powers for good.

Mike O'Meara

Were you really not popular in your own family?

Robb Spewak

I was a loudmouthed kid.

Oscar Santana
You're not shocked by that, are you?

Robb Spewak
Not a rude kid, but a talker. A *constant* talker.

Mike O'Meara
Your family would get frustrated and exasperated with you?

Robb Spewak
My father invented a game. It was called the "Be Quiet Game." We'd be on a road trip, a lengthy car ride for vacation. When you're a kid, 20 minutes is a lengthy car ride. He'd say, "We're going to play a game, and I think you can win this one, Son. It's called the 'Be Quiet Game.' How do you play? You have to be quiet. First person to talk loses."

Mike O'Meara
So you would just yammer in the back of your Dad's station wagon during a family trip?

Robb Spewak
Nothing has changed. Let's say my family was going on a trip; there were many members of my extended family. If we were picking who was riding in what car for the big family caravan, let's just say that I was not the first kid picked for the team.

Mike O'Meara
Who was the member of your family you annoyed the most?

Robb Spewak
Probably my dad.

Oscar Santana
Yeah, he left! He rolled out.

Robb Spewak
He left the marriage.

Mike O'Meara

Do you feel like you're responsible for breaking up your parents' marriage?

Robb Spewak

Well, I was responsible for my parents *getting* married ....

Oscar's World

During each interview I conducted for this book, there was a palpable moment when the other party on the phone began to feel at ease. The gaps between question and corresponding answer narrowed, and I could sense their mental brakes easing, allowing them to speak freely and honestly. I don't mean to suggest that such caution is unwarranted. After all, when a total stranger calls you and asks a litany of personal questions, at some point a voice inside you has to ask, "Is this really a good idea? How sure am I that I can trust this person?" Any sane person would guard themselves and monitor the things they said until they felt reasonably sure they wouldn't regret those decisions. According to this logic, Oscar Santana is a lunatic.

Oscar participated in our conversations the same way he conducts himself on the show: "all in." From the first minute of the first call, he didn't so much *answer* my questions as *react* to them, his verbal knee-jerks to my interrogative reflex hammer. Many of his responses ended with a similar refrain, the too-late qualifying statement "I probably shouldn't have said that." This autonomic reaction, his compulsion to be utterly transparent and unguarded, is equal parts endearing and startling. More than anything else, Oscar wants to portray himself with honesty and sincerity. Nothing else, by comparison, is remotely important to him as a broadcaster.

Oscar Santana

I got into radio for a girl. There was a legendary rock station, 99.1 WHFS, and my high school sweetheart loved the station. I lost her my freshman year in college. I figured the only way to get her back would be to get into radio, and I found college radio for that reason. I got an internship at WHFS simply because I wanted to get that girl back. God bless her for breaking up with me, because it's been the best career.

I was 18, a freshman at Dean College, which is a small two-year university in Franklin, Massachusetts. I went from there to West Virginia University. I somehow convinced my parents that WVU was the school to go to over a handful of other more prestigious universities.

My parents wouldn't pay for an education in broadcasting. They'd only pay for something more traditional, something that they could really understand. In their minds, you go to college to become a doctor, a lawyer, a businessman, or an engineer. I told my mom that WVU was a great school, and it helped that the tuition was not too expensive. I told them I'd be getting an integrated marketing degree from the school of journalism—I didn't tell them the real reason I chose WVU: it had the best radio program.

I worked my way through the college radio ranks and did a morning show on the college station, U92. It was a hip hop show called *The Urban Diner*—not my name for it. It was a staple of U92, popular with young kids and at the state penitentiary up the road, because the inmates could get the radio station there. We'd get letters from prisoners who had song requests. They'd say, "Can you send this out to Cell Block C?"

I had some horrible radio names in college. I started using my real name, Oscar, at WVU, and for the majority of my career I have used Oscar. My last name was changed to Santana a little after we signed with our agent, at his prompting. He insisted that my last name, my proper given name, my God-given name, was too confusing. Zeballos. Was it Greek? Spanish? What was it? He told me I had to change it to something else.

When I tell people this, sometimes they freak out, but it's not like I changed it because I stole a bunch of people's Social Security numbers. It's just that in this business, the people who have great radio names—those aren't their real names. Mike O'Meara is lucky to have a great name with great phonetics. It just screams "superstar."

Mike O'Meara

I've always used my real name. It's always been "Mike O'Meara." I did call myself "Uncle Mike" back at American University, but I always wanted to keep my real name because I was proud of it. It was never an issue because there were never any program directors who approached me about changing my name.

Oscar Santana

Oscar Zeballos is kind of foreign. Sounds like a name from a "do not fly" list at airport security or a watch list at U.S. Immigration. So, "Oscar Santana" was born. The only other name I used during my career was in my freshman year of college. My on-air name was "Maverick," like from the movie *Top Gun*. I am going to throw up. I can't believe I just told you that.

Robb Spewak

Maverick? That's like a porn name!

Oscar Santana

"Request permission for a fly by?" Yeah, request permission to be a douchebag at age 18.

Robb Spewak

I always thought my radio name would be "Jake Stein," because I thought no one would know what to make of "Spewak." No one was going to know how to pronounce it. "Jake Stein" would be a hard one to screw up. He was an actual guy who lived in my father's neighborhood growing up in Carteret, New Jersey, and I love the story that was attached to him. Jake Stein would go into the grocery store with a hammer that he'd use to dent cans. Then he'd ask for a discount on the dented cans.

I swear, my hand to God, that's the truth. A man who buys dented cans—he can't be trusted. However, a man who dents his own cans, well, that's a thinking man.

Oscar Santana

I got internships at WHFS in the summers of my junior and senior years of college. When you're an intern, hanging around, you're trying to get to know the on-air talent, hoping you can trigger a connection to get on the mic. They've got 30, 40, 60 seconds to be on the air unless it's the morning show, so you really have to impress a guy. He doesn't have a lot of time to talk to you before he needs to get to the next Coheed and Cambria or Foo Fighters record, or his program director's going to yell at him. So, I became friends with a morning show. I was your go-to guy. I would do anything to be part of the program, anything to help out, because I really wanted to work in the radio business.

One of the hosts calls me late one night and he says, "We just found out we have a trip to the Bahamas to give away. We're going to do this thing called 'Man Bagging for the Bahamas.' We're going to go on-air, and you have to get into a sleeping bag completely naked. You're going to watch adult movies in the sleeping bag with another completely naked man." I was 22 at the time, and I was like, "Sure! We're going to be on the radio? D.C. radio? Mornings? Why not?" He says, "Great, and there is a benefit for you. You're going to get a trip to the Bahamas, too!" I am thinking to myself, "This is so awesome."

A guy shows up for the promotion. He's in the military and he wants to take his girlfriend on a trip. We both get in the sleeping bag completely naked, ass cheek to ass cheek, but no touching allowed. There were some involuntary grazes, and let me tell you, that was awkward. When you're that young, you forget people are actually listening to the radio. For a month or so after that appearance, I had to field questions about my sexuality from my college friends. It wasn't like, "Oh my God, you got an internship at Capitol Hill and you're working for a congressman or a senator." No, it was, "Hey, you're the naked guy from Man Bagging for the Bahamas."

By the way, I didn't get the trip to the Bahamas. Radio station employees and interns can't win the prizes. I didn't know that, but I am sure they did.

Eventually, I scored my first radio job working with my now-longtime partner Chad Dukes. We raked in a massive $25,000 a year. I can tell you're jealous. It wasn't about the money, though. It was a dream job for me. I remember when I got that gig; I almost wanted to cry. I had just turned 24 and I was doing nights on WHFS—what could go wrong? To answer that question, nine months later the station flipped to Spanish. That went wrong.

By the time I left WJFK a few years later, I'd been through three station flips and one firing. People called us "Big O and Dukes, Station Killers," but that's not quite fair. We just got to stations right before they flipped. I feel like Chad and I had a misconception of what syndication really meant. We just went from city to city—we weren't in multiple cities at the same time. We just kept getting fired.

Robb Spewak

So you thought syndication meant you were heard in many cities, just one at a time?

Oscar Santana

Yeah, we thought every couple of years we'd go to a new city. We didn't know that when you're syndicated, you have to be on in all the cities all at the same time. In retrospect, that seems like it would have been much cooler and less traumatic.

———

Mike O'Meara

One of the things that drives me nuts about Oscar is that he can't quite grasp the English language after spending his entire life in this country. Plus, he doesn't get the pop culture references from 40 or 50 years ago that Robb and I make on a daily basis.

Robb Spewak

Do you think Oscar has ever sat down and watched a black and white movie? No. He told me on the air once he thought the movie *Casablanca* was about the White House. I said, "What are you talking about?" He says, "I'm Spanish, it means 'white house,' so I thought it was about the President." I said, "No! It's Humphrey Bogart! It's the war!" He said, "Aaaah," and just gave me a dismissive hand gesture. He couldn't care less.

It also drives me nuts that Oscar is so much cooler than I am. I go into that three- or four-person studio, and I don't even chart among the top three coolest. I'll never be the guy that's at the hot club with bottle service, hanging out with an NFL player or an iPhone app designer. It's just not me, and it troubles me that he's so much cooler than I am.

Oscar Santana

Of course I am much cooler than Robb. There's no
competition! If cool means being contemporary and he
thinks I make it look easy, he needs to know I am trying hard
every day. I am doing the heavy lifting, and he is just being
himself.

Steve Bridges

When *TMOS* came out to visit KCJJ in Iowa, we learned that
Oscar could connect with anybody. I think he connected
too well with one of our clients, because she cancelled her
account with us. In all fairness to her, she was married, but
anyway ...

Oscar Santana

I promise that I didn't hook up with a married woman. I
would have remembered that. I do remember a few women
that I ran into in Iowa. What a great town.

Robb Spewak

Iowa is a state.

Mike O'Meara

Steve Bridges is a troublemaker! I stand by my teammate.
All I know is that when Oscar Santana got to Iowa, he did a
tremendous amount of charity work, including volunteering
at some of the local homeless shelters.

Oscar Santana

Coven of the Little Sisters. Spent some time there.

Robb Spewak

He cut the ribbon at the hospital. I remember that.

Oscar Santana

Although Downtown Liquors is my favorite place to buy beer
in Iowa.

Robb Spewak

Were you trying to tell a joke there? Did you mean "Liquor Downtown"? Were you trying to say that when you're on a date with a woman in Iowa, you'd love to Liquor Downtown?

Oscar Santana

Damn it!

Robb Spewak

Yes, well done. Almost.

5
THE BEST HAD YET TO COME

Getting laid off was one of the defining moments in my own life. If you've never been fired or laid off from a job, it's hard to explain exactly how it feels to drop your personal effects into a cardboard box while everyone who is still gainfully employed tries to avoid eye contact with you. I don't think my former coworkers viewed me as a leper, as a contagion of unemployment that they feared was communicable. No, to them I was already dead. I was a ghost packing ceramic mugs and unused tea bags to take home to my grave. They only sensed my presence if I accidentally passed too close to them, sending a shiver of icy cold fear down their spines.

You don't realize how much of your self-worth and self-respect is tied to your job until you're fired. You may complain about your daily grind of work stress, but you do not revel in the sudden and complete lack of work stress that accompanies unemployment. Most of us require a regular infusion of cash to stay afloat, to feed our children, to pay our bills, and to stay off the streets. Losing your job is literally life-threatening, and it is a serious blow to everything you believe about yourself. When a company has no qualms telling you that it's better off without you, it's devastating.

In this chapter, we return to the main narrative of the story and explore the day Mike, Robb, and Oscar were laid off from WJFK during its format change. Unfortunately, in an all-too-unstable economy, it's a story with which many readers, perhaps even you, can empathize.

Radio Silence

Oscar Santana

I learned what it means to be fired publically at a very young age, but it was also one of the best things that could have happened to me, to get that experience in my life so early.

As the years passed, and I lost more radio jobs for one reason or another, I always kept my eyes open for the writing on the wall. I was always looking for the station flip. It wasn't a self-fulfilling prophecy or anything, but if you looked carefully, you could see the signs.

You learn the patterns of a station that's going to flip formats. You start understanding what's happening with the sales forecasts and the tempo of your appearances. You pay attention to the packages they're selling for the next quarter. You notice the closed-door meetings. When you see the signs, you have time to prepare yourself. That's how I knew that WJFK would flip before it did.

I am pretty sure I figured it out before Mike and Robb. I knew for a fact it was happening, to a point where I wanted to call Mike to tell him, to give him a heads up. That sucks about radio—you hesitate to tell anybody because you don't know if you can trust anybody. While Mike, Chad, and I were great colleagues, I wasn't working with Mike back then. You never know.

At one point I remember thinking, "We're two or three months away from this happening, so I need to call Mike." I eventually did call but he didn't answer the phone. I left him a message. I didn't tell him in the message; I just told him to give me a call when he got a chance. I should have called him back, but I didn't, so we didn't speak about the flip again until a lot later.

Robb Spewak

I got a call from Mike. It was strange because it was right before the time that I'd get in the car to come to work. I would leave my house around 12:30 or 1:00 p.m., but right around that time the phone rang and it was Mike. "It's over. We're fired. Show's over."

We all had anticipated the news, but still, when you find out, it's a shock. I think I asked Mike, "So what is our next step? What do we do now?" And he said, "Well, we don't go to work today, that's what we do." I hung up the phone, walked up the stairs, sat on my bed, and sighed.

Mike O'Meara

It was not a programming-motivated decision, and I think the ratings demonstrated no significant jump as a result of the change—quite the opposite. What was frustrating was through the entire last three or four months at the radio station, you really got the feeling that they weren't trying to sell it anymore, that somebody knew what was going on. At least that's the impression I got.

They wanted to follow the trends, like radio people do. They figured that sports programming was easier to sell. The way it was explained to me from a sales standpoint is they wanted to sell national advertising through many of the different CBS owned and operated stations, so that they could get a better rate. I was told it was a sales-motivated decision.

Oscar Santana

I try to monitor trends across the country, instead of just looking at my own little sandbox. I watched stations start flipping from the west coast like a tidal wave coming east. Big hot talk stations like KSLX in Los Angeles and KZON in Arizona flipped. Over the next two years, the entire hot talk cluster across the country flipped to something else. I saw that trend coming, and I had a sense it was on its way to us.

Robb Spewak

The station wanted to do a going-away week, one final week of shows, but we weren't into it. For one thing, there was no storied heritage of the show. Mike was a heritage jock, but I wasn't. Not even close! What was I going to do? Celebrate my extremely short stint in the radio business and my subsequent hasty exit? No thanks. At that point, I felt like they had squeezed our oranges dry. They took every last bit of us and our show and squeezed the life out of it. Instead, we produced a final segment that they aired during the final week. We actually started putting elements of it together a few weeks prior, knowing this day was coming.

Transcript of The Final TMOS Broadcast on WJFK: July 17, 2009

The show begins with a mash-up of Star Wars *scenes. In the first, Darth Vader destroys Princess Leia's home planet to demonstrate the power of the Death Star. In the second, Darth Vader and Obi-Wan Kenobi duel; the clip includes a line of dialogue that foreshadows the upcoming announcement: "If you strike me down, I shall become more powerful than you can possibly imagine."*

Cue Music: "It's All Been Done" by the Barenaked Ladies. It's a love song about two people who meet each other over and over again throughout the millennia, repeatedly reincarnated to live out the same dismal existence. They are forever destined to meet, fall in love, and subsequently fall out of love with one another.

It's a whimsical song with ragged emotional undertones about the futility of striving against fate without success. It calls to mind the mythological figure of Sisyphus, doomed forever to push a massive boulder up the steep face of a mountain, only to have it slip through his fingers again and again, just before he reaches the zenith.

Mike O'Meara

CBS and the powers that be, Michael Hughes, C.K., all those good people, gave me the option of coming back and doing one last show for you. I chose to record this message instead of doing that. As I put it to them, I did not want to preside over my own funeral.

If I looked at this as an ending, perhaps it would be appropriate to come in and do a syrupy, sappy last show, but I don't look at it that way. I look at this as a new adventure.

We are done at WJFK. It has been a very, very nice little run for us. As we speak to you, the last ratings that we looked at were the highest that we've had here at WJFK, and we are so, so grateful for that.

People around the country are no strangers to these kinds of circumstances, where you go into work, you're doing your job, you're doing it well, and something like this happens. There are a lot of people who are probably listening to my voice saying, "The same thing happened to me." Unfortunately, in an over 20-year radio career, it's never happened to me before.

We are going to be working behind the scenes to find another home for *The Mike O'Meara Show*. We are going to take some serious time to take a breather and to process all of this. On the air, it's been a delightful year. Behind the scenes, with the economy being what it is, it's been a very difficult year.

We don't predict the future. That's the last thing you can do in show business of any kind, certainly in the radio business. There have been a lot of people that I might say are very talented radio broadcasters who have gone through this exact same thing during this exact same six-month period. You don't know what's going to happen, but I know that I am probably going to be sitting on a beach somewhere for a little while and thinking about how I am chomping at the bit to get back and do this.

That said, it's a very difficult time for entertainment in general, and I think we need to be aware and very vigilant about some of the stuff that is going away. Be aware of how free you are in this country. Be aware of things that are being lost that have any kind of innovation and creativity.

With that said, I think Frank Sinatra sums up where we are in our careers right now ....

Cue the Frank Sinatra song "The Best Is Yet to Come." ▪

Robb Spewak

We wanted to leave it very open-ended. We didn't plan to close up shop and just go home. We wanted to be back as soon as possible. I played that last segment for the last week of shows, keyed the mics off, and left.

Mike O'Meara

Before I got laid off I had never been fired by a radio station. Don and I always left on our own terms. That was a 20-year run without being fired. Prior to that, the last radio gig I had on my own was at WYRE and WPEY in Annapolis, MD. I had resigned at WYRE and the general manager called me into his office. He told me, "This is going to be your last week."

I said, "Neil, I quit already. Now you're telling me it's my last week. I gave you my two-week notice already. If you want me to leave earlier, fine." You get that sometimes in radio and probably a lot of other jobs. You give your two-week notice but they want to have the pleasure of telling you to leave in one week.

Robb Spewak

When I got the official legal papers detailing my termination, the CBS lawyers filed a document that referred to me as a "sidekick." There's actually a piece of legal paper on file somewhere that says, "Robb Spewak, sidekick."

Oscar Santana

Even though my radio partner Chad was retained by WJFK to do a sports show and I was released, I didn't learn of the flip ahead of time from Chad. It wasn't because he was being sneaky or anything like that. Did he tell me as soon as he was approached? I don't think so, but I don't know for sure. I wouldn't expect him to, simply because when you're in that type of conversation or negotiation, until something is 100 percent done, there's no reason to rock the boat.

By the time he hinted at it, I had already heard from somebody else. I knew enough people, and I was a good enough guy, that somebody gave me a heads up.

Robb Spewak

One of our affiliates in Iowa, KCJJ, is run by a man named Steve Bridges. He had carried *The Don and Mike Show*, he carried *The Mike O'Meara Show*, and he was actually one of the ones that kept me employed—at least briefly—after the show was dropped.

Steve Bridges

When I picked up *The Don and Mike Show* way back and they announced us as a new affiliate, Don said, "Of all the rinky-dink stations we're on, this is the rinky-dinkiest." Mike tried for a minute to stand up for us, but then he just gave up. They were absolutely right, but I loved it. KCJJ *was* rinky-dink. They called it like they saw it.

Hell, when I started carrying them, I was running the board. When I bought this station, it was in bad shape, 1000 watts. We've got a huge signal now, but not back then. I was running the boards, and it was a mess. They knew it was a mess.

The network said if I'd buy the satellite, they'd give me the show, but I said, "I can't buy the satellite, I don't have $3,000. I want you to give me the satellite." I fought with the network for two months. They finally gave me the satellite because they wanted the affiliates. I can be persuasive at times.

Robb Spewak

Steve called me. He is a funny guy, a grizzled radio guy. I had spoken maybe 15 words to him in over 20 years. I picked up the phone and there he was like we were old friends.

"Hey! This is Steve out at KCJJ. Listen, the network says that if I don't ride them out for 30 days of *The Mike O'Meara Show* they'll give me a replacement show in perpetuity free of charge." I said, "You're kidding!" They just wanted us gone.

He said, "My contract says I get 30 episodes, so I'm getting 30 episodes." I said, "You know you are keeping me employed." He said, "Yeah, for four weeks."

So he knew and he was very nice about it. He stuck to his guns and he kept *TMOS* on his station. I think there were only two affiliates aside from WJFK that kept us on until the bitter, and I mean bitter, end.

The last *Mike O'Meara Show* was in July, but I was retained until August in order to deliver the last 30 days of "best of" clip shows. I produced them from my house. I would cut them together and then upload the finished files to CBS in New York City. Each day, I'd upload a new show and each day was one day closer to the end. I remember uploading the final one and thinking, "Once I hit 'send,' I am going to be brought into the office and fired." I figured it wouldn't take them long.

It was late afternoon on a Friday when I uploaded the final show, so I figured I'd probably get dragged into the office on Monday. Nope—they called me right away. The phone rang at 2:45 p.m. that Friday, and they asked me to come by the station. I thought, "You're going to fire me two hours before the close of business on a Friday?" but what I really said was, "Yeah, it'd be great to come in right now." They fired me 25 minutes after I turned in the last piece of work I was contractually obligated to do. Not only did they not "need me anymore," they wanted me out of there as fast as possible.

Mike O'Meara

It's very difficult to hold your head high and go into a radio station on a daily basis when you know you're doing the best job you can but the people who are supposed to sell the airtime for your show aren't really motivated to go out and do that. A few of them probably know what's happening before you do. It's an excruciatingly difficult environment. I wouldn't describe it as pressure. I would describe it as a total feeling of abandonment, and that's the most painful thing that I experienced when I was dealing with the format change at WJFK. It made for a miserable time for everybody.

Carla O'Meara

It was just awful because Mike was thinking, "I did a bad job and that's why I got cancelled." At the moment, that's all he could think, regardless of all the business-related decisions behind the scenes.

Robb Spewak

There was a lot of emotion, for sure. If you've had a gun held to your head for four months, it's almost better for them to pull the trigger.

Mike O'Meara

When I finally got the confirmation that they were making the change, it was almost a relief.

Robb Spewak

After that many years of loyal service, it was honestly very strange to feel relieved that I got fired, but I don't think I ever got really emotional. It's not like I got hit by a car, out of the blue. Instead it's like I knew I was going to get hit by a car, and I was standing out in the street wondering, "When is that car going to get here?"

I remember feeling very unhappy coming to work at the station, and what makes it worse is that I was there when it was still a great station. A fun place to work, an important station, a heritage station. I loved being a part of it.

Then, over time, I watched it erode and decay. It took years to decay to the dismal workplace it became. It was like watching a loved one with a terminal illness. There's nothing you can do. You're powerless, and you're watching something you love slip away. It's just sad.

Oscar Santana

The whole thing sucked, but I wanted to go out with a big smile on my face. I wanted to celebrate the show that was *Big O and Dukes*. I wasn't going to rant and rave: "How dare you not give me a shot to succeed? How dare you break up the team? What's going to happen to me?" Wasn't going to do that.

There was a possibility of a job at WPGC; that was intimated to me, but I knew that the job was going to be a long shot because that's not what I wanted to do with my life. I wanted more than that. I knew I could offer more than just *that*. And not to disrespect anyone who does music radio; it's an art form, but I knew I had more to offer than just to go to another music station.

I wanted to go out with my head held high. I was proud of what we had accomplished together, what I had accomplished myself, individually. It was a good run, you know?

I didn't have any hard feelings that they kept Chad and dumped me. I've always rooted for his success. In a weird way, I was proud of him. I knew that he was taking on an entirely different genre. He was doing a really different show with someone he'd never worked with before, and when I started listening to his show, I knew they had the right guy for the job. With all due respect to LaVar Arrington, the former Washington Redskin and his new cohost, LaVar was just learning how to be a broadcaster. They had the right guy there to teach him how to do a great show.

I'm not a sports guy and that's what they wanted. I tried to become one in that last year of our show, but it just wasn't me.

I wouldn't have felt comfortable walking in there every day and stressing out if I didn't know what a 3–4 defense was or if I was going to fumble over what Alexander Ovechkin's stats were the day before. That's not my passion.

Mike Kelley
Was that a pun?

Oscar Santana
What do you mean?

Mike Kelley

"Fumbling" over stats because you aren't a sports guy?

Oscar Santana

Not an intentional pun, no. You see? That's exactly why I wouldn't be good on sports radio. I didn't get my own joke.

Facing the Final Curtain

Mike O'Meara

Getting canned hurt. It hurt because we built a really solid following. Even after Don left, we continued to do a terrific radio program and we continued to have very, very good ratings. We were doing what we were expected to do, but I got the feeling that no matter what we did, the new format was going to happen regardless.

Oscar Santana

At one point after the layoff I was at a barbeque at my parents' house, and my mother asked, "What's going on? You seem sad, like something bad happened." I said, "Actually, I'm happy. I can walk around knowing that I worked as hard as I could. I put everything I could into my show, and now I just need to find the next opportunity. I need to keep grinding to be prepared for it."

Robb Spewak

It was difficult to communicate how I felt to the rest of my family. They have what I would classify as "more standard" work. Sales jobs—you know, Joe jobs. To be in "show business" was foreign to my family. Where I was from, the patriarch started a furniture store and everyone worked for him. It probably sounds like *Leave It to Beaver* or something, but what are you going to do? That's how it was. Sell things and come home—that was the mindset. I wouldn't say they looked down on me because of the job I'd chosen; they sort of looked at me sideways. My parents knew what I did for a living, and they could understand how much time I spent and how hard I worked, but my extended family, not so much.

That probably motivated me to some degree. I wanted to get out there and succeed, to show them. They don't really say it out loud, but you get a clear sense when someone is not, let's say, overly impressed with your choice of career. When it all came apart, it was rough. For my entire adult life, I had worked basically one job for one company at one location. I had worked there unpaid, earned my keep as a part-timer, and had finally graduated to working on a quality program that I cohosted. And then I got fired. When you're doing your best work, and you know you can't possibly be working any harder, and they fire you, it hurts. You feel like you haven't done enough, but then again, you can't figure out what else you could possibly have done.

When I look back on the show and my history at the station, I can say this: The only thing we ever did was everything they asked us to do. You do that for years and years, and then it's still not enough.

If I had to give advice to someone about how to handle being laid off, I would tell them to look from the outside-in for a moment. My original reaction, my first thought was, "What did I do wrong?" Look from the outside instead of blaming yourself automatically. If you did your job and circumstances out of your control got you fired—if you did your part and still got canned, screw them. You didn't get fired because of something you did or didn't do. In my case, I always gave 100 percent, being as funny and as charming as I am capable of, so there's nothing more I could have done. Amazingly, my charm did not save the hot talk format.

Anyway, if you can look from the outside-in, objectively, and know that it's not your fault, then don't beat yourself up about it. I had a lot of good years working there—not everything was terrible, especially not at first, and I don't regret one single minute of it. Toward the end, when I spent most of the day wondering if I'd have a job, it stopped being fun, and I blamed myself for it. It took me a while to figure out that it wasn't my fault that the station went the way it did.

Oscar Santana

When I was 26 or 27 years old, I remember sitting in a meeting for *The Big O and Dukes Show* in Baltimore, the last year we were on the station. We had a consultant there, and I was under the impression that everyone in the room who we were meeting with, including the vice president of programming, the general manager, and a radio station consultant, were there to help me improve my craft. I was open to that—no big deal. I didn't know everything; I was learning, cutting my teeth.

It quickly became obvious that the meeting was all about how they wanted us to change our show. It wasn't about us learning—it was about them telling us what we were going to do to stay on the air there. I basically cursed out all of management and accused them of lying to us. I told them they should have let us stay at our last radio station instead of hiring us just to screw up our show in Baltimore. That began the demise of our run at 105.7 WHFS. I'll always remember that, because I look back at my reaction and think, "That probably wasn't the smartest decision I have ever made."

You realize at certain points in your life that it doesn't matter how talented you think you are or what you think you have to offer. You're not the boss, and you're not the owner of wherever you're broadcasting from. That makes you an employee, and everybody's replaceable. If somebody wants you out, you're out.

Robb Spewak

Especially toward the end, WJFK was not a very pleasant environment for a show like ours. So much censorship, so much fretting and worry. It's hard to be funny when you have to think twice before you say anything—it kills the spontaneity. It causes you to second-guess yourself, and under those circumstances you just cannot do your best work.

The environment is lousy, but you deal with it. You come in every day, you do your best work, and then one day it's all over. I was 38, married, a father of two, a homeowner, and now unemployed. I got fired from the one thing I do better than anything else, so where do you go from there?

I remember having lunch with someone from management. I told him, "I have worked for the station for 15 years. I can do *everything*—any job—in that building. I understand that the station is changing formats, but is there anything I can do in this new incarnation of the radio station? Is there any place left for me?"

His answer was cold and utterly dismissive. I still remember exactly what he said: "We won't be needing you anymore." That hurts, man. I gave an awful lot to that station, sweat equity over a long period of time, and all I wanted was some sort of job—anything so that I could keep the lights on and feed my family. But no, they had nothing for me. At the end, I diminished myself, diminished what I was capable of, to try and keep some semblance of a job, and they rejected even that. It felt rotten, and it also made me really disappointed in myself. I felt like I wasn't able to provide for my family because I wasn't able to make a living.

Oscar Santana

Especially because of my ... regrettable decisions in Baltimore, I figured out how to pick myself up when things like this happen. I think an entrepreneurial spirit lives in me because the most fun part of the process is building—building a business, the show. Then you move to sustaining, but for me the fun is creating. That's why I love being part of *The Mike O'Meara Show* so much. Every day we're creating; there is no status quo. There's no end to the creativity—no day is ever the same.

Mike O'Meara

I never would have wanted to stay through the format change at WJFK. They never even had a conversation with me about it. I have no idea what the powers-that-be were thinking but there was never, ever a discussion about putting me on in any kind of sports capacity whatsoever.

I think they had the characters they wanted in place and I was not among them. I was capable of doing sports interviews. I did sports interviews when I was on The Edge; I did sports interviews on WJFK. However, I wouldn't want to be handcuffed, forced to talk sports analysis every day. I would have put a shotgun in my mouth.

Robb Spewak

No surprise, I am not a fit at a sports station.

Oscar Santana

The whole time *Big O and Dukes* was on WJFK, until about the last two or three months of the show, we were trying to be the sports show we thought we needed to be to stay on the air. We had almost all sports guests, but it was a double-edged sword, because the persona I built on the show wasn't really a sports guy. In real life, I'm not really a sports guy either.

What's weird is that I have a lot of friends who are athletes—real friends. My good friend Dominique Foxworth is the President of the NFL Players Association. As the first generation of my family in this country, my parents didn't really foster much of a love of sports. If sports were ever on television in the house, it was just soccer. That meant I had to foster an interest in sports on my own, and I did. In an interesting twist of fate, I am more of a sports fan right now than I have ever been, but that doesn't mean I want to talk about it for four or five hours a day. Maybe that's just me.

Dealing with Downtime

Mike Kelley

What did you do after the layoff? What happened in the interim between the radio show ending and the podcast beginning?

Robb Spewak

Well, I did a lot of sitting for a few months. It was strange; having worked for Don and Mike for years, I was used to downtime. The guys got a lot of vacation time. I, on the other hand, did not. I was an employee, but when the show was on holiday, essentially, so was I. I'd drive in to work, sit at my desk, do a crossword puzzle, and after I was sure that management saw that I was there, boom! Out the door.

I lived for vacation. When I got my long breaks, like at Christmastime, when I could finagle two weeks or so, I would love every second of that time off. However, 48 hours after I was fired? I was restless. I was itching for something to do, missing that creative outlet. I was going out of my mind. It was maddening. Like I said, I'd had stretches of time with not much to do, but never for an open-ended segment of time. I still had a severance package, and I still had insurance through the company for a few months, but it only took two or three days until I started pacing.

Steve Bridges called me up again during our downtime. Same greeting: "Hey." He asked, "What do you want to do now?" I said I'd like to play records. He said "OK, you want Friday afternoons?" Of course I did! "OK, you can have it." And that's how my music show started on KCJJ. It was a real lifesaver for me. It gave me purpose—something to do.

Steve Bridges

Robb does a great job with his music show, but there are times that I want to kill him. I'm trying to run an AM station that's supposed to be hip and adult contemporary, and Robb plays Henry Mancini from some movie that I never goddamn heard of. He's not playing "Moon River" or even a Mancini B-side, more like an E- or an F-side. Even if this doesn't go into the book, please remind Robb that I can't have Henry Mancini on the station anymore.

Mike O'Meara

I really enjoyed the break I got after the layoff in the fall and winter of 2009. That was, believe it or not, a very pleasant time because suddenly I had an opportunity to take a breather, reflect, and enjoy myself. I maximized the time I had off and said yes to a few things I may never have if I were working. I did what I wanted to do; I rode my motorcycle.

Of course, you can only be content being idle for so long, and then you want to get going again. I was ready in December of 2009 to start broadcasting again, and I was ready to return to radio.

Robb Spewak

Mostly what I remember at that time is drinking a lot. There was never any reason to get up early or to go to bed at any sensible time. You think, "Another drink? Sure, why not?" My wife was extraordinarily supportive, and my kids were the best. When I was laid off, I think they and I sort of had an understanding. We both knew that, for the next few months, we were going to spend a lot of time together. I did some volunteering at their school. It was neat because not a lot of dads get to do that. Most dads—including me, at least for a while there—have to work when their kids are in school. I got a chance to see them during the day, in their own natural habitat.

Because my job meant so much to me, when things weren't going well at the station, and then during the layoff, I probably internalized it. That made me a little distant emotionally. I probably should have allowed more time for the kids. Even though I did lots of stuff with them between jobs, I could have done more. I should have stopped and thought, "This is a real opportunity to be the best dad of all time." It was hard, though, to fight that sinking feeling deep down, that feeling that being out of work was really bad. I wish I had made better use of that downtime.

Oscar Santana

When you know you're getting fired, you start looking for different options. I got fired on a Friday and I had a meeting at another radio station, WPGC 95.5 FM, on Monday. I understood that they may have had a job opportunity for me.

I met the program director, who started talking to me about being a DJ on WPGC. He told me that WPGC was going to turn into a Top 40 station, so they were looking for some diversity. They needed a Latin guy, because it couldn't just be an African-American station.

So I was thinking I'd be the Ryan Seacrest of Washington, D.C.; I'd talk about Ke$ha and Fall Out Boy and all those bands. I'm already a fan of that music, so it could have been a good opportunity for me. However, I quickly realized that wasn't the case. The program director told me, "We'd like you to live 'The Lifestyle.'" I said, "Excuse me? The Lifestyle?" And he said, "Yeah, we have a very urban lifestyle here." He had no idea who I was, but he'd been told to interview me for this gig. He was going to hire me because he was told he had to by some corporate higher-up.

He saw a Latin guy and thought I was Mr. Hip Hop. He wanted me to start wearing FUBU, Iceberg, and flat-brimmed hats. He clearly had no idea what I had to offer; I could offer a lot more than The Lifestyle. So I told him, "Alright, I'll give you a call tomorrow to set everything up," and I walked out. I made a quick call in the a.m. to say thank you but no thank you and peace out.

I didn't want anyone to try to turn me into DJ Flex when I'm fine with who I am. That wouldn't be a terrible thing, because DJ Flex does very well, but Oscar Santana is no DJ Flex. To be honest, if roles were reversed, I don't think he wants to be a talk show host either. So my brief, 24-hour stint at WPGC ended, and I thought, "I have a pretty good network of people, consulting and marketing-wise," and one of those gentlemen happened to be my future boss, Evan McConnell. I reached out to him.

I told him, "I know you own a mobile computer lab company. I'm thinking of a career change. This is my business background. Do you have any opportunities we could talk about?" He invited me to his home, we sat in the back of his house, and we started talking. He asked me to come by the office, and the next thing you know I was hired. Within the next six or seven months, I worked my way up to vice president of marketing. I was out of work for approximately 26 days, less than a month.

Mike Kelley
You were still working off of a severance, then?

Oscar Santana
Severance? Please! Are you kidding me? Severance? That was two weeks. I had one more paycheck coming. Oh, man.

Mike Kelley

You broadcasted for five hours a day until you were laid off, and all you got was your final paycheck?

Oscar Santana

Yeah. It's a kick in the neck. Every time we signed a contract, they told us the *next* time would be the contract when we'd write our own check for any amount we wanted. But that next contract never got there because hot talk died, at least for now. I think it's bound to make a big comeback.

Robb Spewak

I worked for WJFK for 19 years, and working there was all I knew how to do. Thank God the podcast happened, so I was able to continue in the same line of work. I never really did anything except *The Mike O'Meara Show*, and before that *The Don and Mike Show*. If the podcast hadn't happened, I really never had a plan B.

6

DEAD AIR:
THE STATE OF RADIO

Why does the human mind insist on capturing and reliving the worst, most tragic, moments of our lives in vivid detail? Do you remember where you were when you heard about planes smashing into the World Trade Center? How about the explosion of the Space Shuttle? Less tragic, but arguably more bone-chilling: Do you remember Dennis Franz exposing his naked bottom during a sex scene on the television series *NYPD Blue*? Undulating nudity in the form of incomprehensible Franzian topography had shimmied its way onto prime time, and our retinas would never be the same.

It's hard to remember a time when radio was as controversial, challenging its listeners and redefining culture. Whereas television and movies continue to entice us, radio has given up. We stampede into theaters to see shocking films, and we binge watch groundbreaking television programs. Radio, once a powerful medium, is now the soundtrack for the dentist's office, mindlessly tittering to itself, fully aware that no one is listening. Gone are the days of appointment radio, when huge personalities ruled the airwaves. We're left with stale, safe, unimaginative programming that is so formulaic and automated that DJs are no longer required. After all, a computer can run a playlist and never miss a commercial break.

In this chapter, we lament the death of good radio and conduct a post-mortem on its untimely demise.

Don't Touch That Dial

Steve Bridges

Radio is all I ever wanted to do since I was four years old. My dad would get the radio down from the cupboard when my brothers were asleep, and we'd sit in the kitchen listening to the disc jockeys—I was drawn to them. I never wanted to do anything else. I wanted to talk on the radio; I wanted to be like those disc jockeys: Don Steele, Larry Lujack.

Those guys made personal connections. *The Don and Mike Show* did the same thing. They talked to people, to the listeners. They weren't shilling; they weren't fake. They were *real*. Just like the disc jockeys I grew up with.

I idolized Dick Clark, whom I got to meet and work with a little bit. You compare Dick Clark with Mike O'Meara, and you ask where the connection is. Here it is: they're real. When you watched Dick Clark on TV, that was Dick Clark. That's who he really was, and he translated. Not everybody's real on TV or radio, but they can translate enough of themselves so you know that's the actual person, and you like that person. If you don't like someone, you might listen for novelty but not for loyalty.

Oscar Santana

Radio is the hardest medium to communicate and really connect with someone in. You're not in front of a camera. Listeners can't hear facial expressions. They can't see what you're doing. You have to explain it to them, and they have

82

to hear the sincerity in your voice in order to buy in. I always thought that if you could do that, it was almost like magic.

Arch Campbell

Radio has changed so tremendously. Now almost everything is talk and news. I miss the days of music radio, when there were maybe three or four formats, but everybody pretty much listened to the same kinds of music. At this point, AM radio is dead. FM is still alive, but there's not a lot of music I want to listen to, and there aren't many shows that look anything like *The Mike O'Meara Show*. They just don't exist anymore.

Mike O'Meara

When WJFK flipped, sports talk was the flavor of the month, one of many that come and go in radio. There aren't a lot of original ideas, not a lot of innovation in radio. What you get is a lot of people who end up doing the exact same thing. That is why now when you look at most major markets you will have right-wing talk, you will have sports talk, you will have urban music, you will have classic rock, and you will have country.

Guy talk, as a format, was destroyed—blown up. Why? I think because it wasn't as advertiser-friendly as the sports talk format. It's much easier for radio salespeople to walk into a car dealership and say, "Buy ads on our station, because we're going to talk about the Redskins all day, and you can just leave the station on in the background." It's harder to say, "Buy some time on this radio station because one guy is going to talk about his vasectomy while the other one talks about Bill Cosby."

Robb Spewak

I think radio is in a period now when they will gladly accept lower ratings if it costs less to do it. Why not replace a DJ with some younger, hungrier guy who will work for half the money, no benefits, and no vacation time? It's become a bottom-line financial thing. That leads to an amazing amount of turnover. Loyalty doesn't matter when you're running a radio station.

Tony Perkins

Radio has lost touch with its listeners. I think it has become a much more corporate, play-by-the-numbers, play-it-safe kind of medium. Some of what's happened to radio has not been radio's fault—it's just the advance of new technology. But I believe that radio, many years ago, started doing itself in by tightening playlists and devaluing personalities.

Any radio that stands out now is still personality-driven, but radio doesn't value that anymore. The pay scales have dropped tremendously, and they will never go back to what they were because the whole business model is out of whack now. Radio hastened its own demise by being less interesting, less fun, more predictable, and bland.

Mike O'Meara

Don and I were very blessed to have some very lucrative contracts for a long time. I have no regrets about that. I don't feel any bitterness about a radio station wanting to improve its bottom line. What I miss more than the money is how cool it used to be when you were on the radio. It was *the* place to be.

When they let me go, they wanted to get rid of some of the larger salaries at the station. In the landscape of sports talk, there aren't a lot of superstars, but there are a lot of guys who are happy to flap their gums about sports all day long. And you don't have to pay them as much.

Arch Campbell

You don't have to pay for top talent anymore because there are so many choices. I think the most money I ever made in my career was 25 years ago, in the early 1990s. In those days, you'd actually earn a talent fee if you appeared as a guest on someone's television or radio show. Now you do it for free because there just isn't any money.

These days big companies own most of the stations. Let's say Clear Channel, for example, owns six or seven radio stations in the Washington, D.C. market. They don't need to compete anymore; they don't need to be the top-rated station. Because of all the stations they own, combined, they can be rated second and third, and that's enough. Individual radio stations don't have to be the best, they just have to be good enough as a package.

Steve Bridges

You don't have people in radio anymore who remember what the hell radio was. It was immediate, it was personal, and it was local. You can even have a national show and it can be local. Local means connecting with your listeners. Now you have a bunch of kids that just got out of marketing classes, and they don't remember what radio was. They don't remember where the magic was, and they don't have respect for it.

These corporations bought up all these radio stations and overleveraged themselves. They cost their stockholders a ton of money in the beginning and got rid of all the talent. It'd be like if somebody bought Ford, got rid of the F-150, and made a pedal car instead. The thing that made those stations valuable—the personalities, the local feel, the interaction, and the loyalty? They got rid of all of that because they couldn't afford to buy all those stations at once. It's a travesty, and the only reason Mike and those guys aren't on a network is cost. People don't want to pay them.

Tony Perkins

As an audience gets more fragmented, you're fighting for a smaller piece of the pie. I can name a dozen radio personalities who were stars in their markets when I was growing up. Their shows were inventive. They had their own styles, they did their own thing. They would go out and host a concert for the Commodores or Journey and people would be almost as excited to see that DJ as they would the act.

As those stars grew and salaries got bigger, some other costs started to grow and the amount of pie you could attract got smaller. They tried to control their operating costs, but when you do that, the talent starts jumping ship. As far as I am concerned, you get what you pay for. If you can only pay for a mid-level, bland disc jockey or television reporter, then you're going to get what you pay for, and it becomes a self-fulfilling prophecy. The ratings drop.

It's become less about chasing the big ratings and more about living with an acceptable rating level with a certain profit margin.

Mike O'Meara

As long as I've been doing radio, there's always been an ongoing battle between the sales department and the programming department. Unfortunately, money talks and the sales departments are winning. Safe, non-controversial, sameness is winning. You're getting what the general managers, sales managers, and sales executives think should be on the air. They base it on what is trendy that won't rock the boat too much. They are looking to deliver the safest, least controversial programming to maximize advertiser dollars.

Right-wing talk does very well among large numbers of people. Sports talk does very well among advertisers. What's gone is any sense of originality. You don't get a Howard Stern, or anyone creating new, exciting stuff. You get three different stations talking about the same football game in the least imaginative way possible—just yack, yack, yack, yack, yack. It's terrible.

Tony Perkins

Every day on our morning television broadcast, we show some viral video. For the most part, why have those videos gone viral? Because they're wild, or there's something out of the norm about them. They are people taking risks, doing something unusual. That is still what gets the attention, but corporate broadcasters are so afraid of offending anybody or turning off somebody that they dumb it down, they make it blander. In effect, they blow off the audience.

People have so many options now, why listen to something so incredibly dull? Nowadays on the radio, a song will play and a DJ will come on with a 12- to 14-second tidbit: "Don't know if you heard about Miley Cyrus at the CMAs. Boy, that was a fail. Can't believe that happened." Then it's onto the next song. That's their "personality" now: 12 seconds. You get a whole lot more personality from a single 20-minute segment on the Mike O'Meara podcast.

Steve Bridges

When I had *The Don and Mike Show* on, I had a 29 share on KCJJ. When WJFK pulled the plug on *The Mike O'Meara Show*, I thought ... uh oh. But when Mike's podcast went on, we had a 30 share; it was right there and never dropped. I have no idea why stations won't carry their podcast. It's always been a great show, a compelling show.

I have talked to stations—most of them are group ownerships. I haven't found Mom and Pops. They don't know how to handle *TMOS*. I don't get it. The show should be on a bunch of stations—it really should be. It's a good show, and radio is shortchanging itself by not carrying it.

I am pretty sure that if I didn't own my radio station, I would have been fired by now. Mike and I are cut out of the same cloth. We have stuff to say, and it doesn't fit what corporations want to do now. It's not political and it's not sports. As far as music stations, they're all automated. I don't run the station like that. I've got live people still. It costs a lot of money, but I'm a dinosaur.

Now Appearing

Even in its glory days, radio still had its downside. One of the biggest headaches for DJs then and now is the dreaded radio appearance. Built into a commercial sell, these appearances obligated DJs to appear at the client's location, usually for hours at a time. "We're broadcasting live in the parking lot of Herman's Hermit Crabs Pet Store Supply Warehouse. Come on out to see us for a free bumper sticker and a 15 percent off coupon for birdseed, from 10 a.m. to 7 p.m. today only!"

I asked Mike, Robb, and Oscar to discuss their most memorable appearances and station-sponsored radio stunts.

Robb Spewak

I've done dozens of appearances where I showed up and the merchant didn't know I was going to be there, because that's how they handled things at WJFK. I had to explain that I was going to be in their store for two hours. One time I had to pretend to call in and be live on the air to fool the store owner, because it was promised to him that I would do a phone-in.

My worst appearance ever was three consecutive Saturdays washing people's windshields at a gas station. It was never promoted as, "This is Robb from *The Don and Mike Show* washing your windows!" I was just washing windows. That's it.

Mike O'Meara

Like a homeless man. A squeegee boy!

Robb Spewak

They gave me a gas station attendant shirt to wear, so people probably thought I was a gas station employee. I think it was a lateral promotion to go from disc jockey to washing windows.

Oscar Santana

When you're pumping gas, the last thing you want is someone approaching you and saying, "Hey! Would you like a T-shirt?" No, I just want to pump my gas and leave.

My worst promotion was when the D.C. sniper was at large and I was working at WHFS. It was a year before WHFS flipped to Spanish, and they were trying to do anything they could for press. They put the promotions team out, right next to DC101, with a big balloon at a gas station. We had to go pump gas for listeners. The press release read, "We'll take a bullet for our listeners." This is while the sniper was still shooting people, mind you.

Robb Spewak

Someone probably got a tremendous pat on the back for that.

Oscar Santana

We were out there for two hours pumping gas. I was just figuring, well, if it's my time to die, it's my time to die. Everyone was wearing helmets, like they were going to stop a bullet.

I remember going home afterward and telling my mom about it. She asked me, "What are you doing with your life?"

Mike O'Meara

That's the best part of the story: "What are you doing with your life?"

Robb Spewak

I think we've all had parents and grandparents who asked us that question.

Mike O'Meara

I had to go to one of those big-box electronics retail stores and sit in a parking lot. Four people came. I said to myself, "This is over. My radio days of pulling a thousand people at an appearance are over." I think one guy said, "Hey, are you Mike?" I said, "Yeah." He said, "I brought my kid out to see the fire trucks." That was the bottom for me. I frigging hated it.

I'd done remotes down at WYRE in Annapolis when I started my career, and there I was again, but not even live on the air. I was just sitting there, doing an in-store appearance. I did a lot of those because I needed the money, the appearance fees. Once, they sent me out to a wireless phone store for two hours. I remember wanting to say, "If we get 12 people at this store, I'll give you each $20 and you can go into the dollar store next door and buy whatever you want." Every appearance I did when I was at 105.9 The Edge—except for my motorcycle ride—was the worst appearance I ever did.

Radio and Yard Sales

If good radio is "immediate, personal, and local," then *The Mike O'Meara Show* podcast is better than most modern radio. What could be more immediate, personal, and local than preparing for a yard sale? In one of the most memorable *TMOS* episodes, Mike comes to terms with his new economic reality, pricing items that will be strewn about his lawn the following morning. This is not the kind of radio that can be squeezed into a 12-second segment.

Robb Spewak

Because we are just "us," just a group of guys and not a show on a station owned by a company owned by a conglomerate, I think we are able to be goofier now. There's less structure, fewer restrictions. We can do specialty shows like a wine tasting show that is less about wine tasting and more about wine drinking.

One of my favorite shows ever was Mike preparing for his first yard sale in Manassas, and we took an entire episode to price the items. I found it very entertaining when I listened back to it, because it was an instance of us doing our best to be entertaining in a situation that would never present itself in real show business.

Mike O'Meara

I think the most entertaining shows that we do on *TMOS* come out of something real. They are always organic. Maybe something happens because we are recording a show at a Christmas party and someone's had a little bit too much to drink. With the yard sale, for example, it was totally organic. I was bringing stuff down from my attic. I am no longer getting paid a radio salary that allows me to keep all this stuff, so I have to start making money any way I can.

Robb, with his family of retail geniuses, has priced yard sale items his whole life. He's had many different yard sales but I hadn't. Carla's bringing all of this merchandise into the living room and Robb is pricing it, because at 5 a.m. the next day, we had to drag everything out to the front yard. It was funny, but it was real. Plus all of us were drinking Honey Crisp Apple Sangrias for the whole show.

Mike O'Meara

Before I start bringing the stuff in here, I wanted to mention my emotions about the yard sale. I'm swimming with varied emotions, of course.

Oscar Santana

Why?

Mike O'Meara

I'll tell you why, Oscar, and this may sound a little elitist. It was not five years ago, perhaps even less than that—perhaps a year and a half ago—a yard sale was not in my ... future.

Oscar Santana

Wasn't in your tax bracket.

Robb Spewak

Not five years ago you would just as soon throw the stuff away than try to make a dollar off of it.

Mike O'Meara

All this stuff would have been in Goodwill. Now I'm saying to myself, "This stuff has value. Put it on the front lawn. A great American tradition."

Robb Spewak

This is money in your pocket; this is you cleaning out your house.

Light music sets the ambience, a jazz interpretation of The Price is Right *theme song. Carla O'Meara begins to bring items into the studio, like one of Barker's Beauties. Mike intermittently refers to her as Vanna White.*

Mike O'Meara

Carla, can you please bring the first item up for bid on *The Price is Right*?

Carla brings out a lamp.

Oscar Santana

Ooooooh! Look at this thing!

Robb Spewak

Is that a working lamp? You'll want to have an extension cord tomorrow so you can prove that it works.

Mike O'Meara

He's so good at this.

Robb Spewak

Just run an extension cord outside. I would say you could get $35 for that as long as it's complete. I may even go higher but I'd take $35.

Mike O'Meara

The next item is a fully-packaged herb garden.

Robb Spewak

Do you know what you paid for that, retail?

Carla O'Meara

Over $200.

Robb Spewak

Boy, that's tough.

Mike O'Meara

It was a gift.

Oscar Santana

A wedding gift ... from me.

Robb Spewak

I would price that at $60, but be ready to take a hit on it.

Oscar Santana

No!

Robb Spewak

Price it at $60, and remember to be less eager to bargain earlier than later.

Mike O'Meara

Moving right along. What's next?

Robb Spewak

An exercise mat. That's not going to bring much money, because everyone's stuck with stuff like that. I would say put $5 on that.

Oscar Santana

I'll buy that for $5 right now. Sold.

Robb Spewak

I should have said $10.

Mike O'Meara

Next is a yoga ball.

Oscar Santana

A stability ball. New, they're like $20–$30.

Robb Spewak

Then $8. If it's something like new, mark it one-third of retail.

Oscar Santana

But who's been working out on that ball?

Mike O'Meara

I have.

Robb Spewak
Then $4.

Oscar Santana
You should sign that ball! You could get $20 for it.

Mike O'Meara
You know what? No. Next is an ionized air purifier.

Robb Spewak
Sharper Image?

Carla O'Meara
Brookstone.

Robb Spewak
Does it come with a sticker that says "jackass"? You might be able to trick someone into paying $40 for that.

Oscar Santana
Like the elderly. My mom has five of those in her home. Ooooo, next is some clothing.

Robb Spewak
A leather sex vest.

Mike O'Meara
A leather *biker* vest. Never been worn.

Robb Spewak
A top-notch Harley Davidson vest, laced on the side for venting, like new. You shouldn't take a penny under $40.

Mike O'Meara
What do we have here? A rice steamer?

Robb Spewak
It's never been used?

Carla O'Meara

Once.

Robb Spewak

I get fluky on food stuff that's been used, so I'd say it's never been used. $10. I have a rice steamer, and I've used it maybe three times. It's not a useful thing.

Buzz Burbank

Next is a telescope.

Robb Spewak

Now, Mike, when I told you that you needed a sexy item, this is a sexy item.

Buzz Burbank

This is your lead item right here.

Robb Spewak

This is a great item. Put this close to the sidewalk, because this is going to draw people in. I'd say you start that at $120, and I'd pay $120 for that if I needed a telescope. How much does that retail for? $300?

Mike O'Meara

What's the brand name on that, Carla?

Robb Spewak

Kirkland.

Carla O'Meara

It's Meade.

Buzz Burbank

That's a very good brand!

Oscar Santana

Are you feeling better about the yard sale, Mike?

Mike O'Meara

I knew this would work, with you and Robb and Buzz. This gives me so much more confidence going into tomorrow.

Robb Spewak

And the next item shares Mike's old nickname: "Swiss Therapy Balls." Brand new in box. We said $8 on the one that's open, so we go $10 on the one in the box. People love stuff new-in-box.

Oscar Santana

What do those balls do?

Mike O'Meara

I use it for my back—I lean on it. And Carla and I have sex on it.

Oscar Santana

Can I buy that? ▪

———

Carla O'Meara

I am so done with yard sales. Let me tell you that. I am so finished. Looking back at that first yard sale, I didn't believe Robb's prices, so we priced everything too high. What I've realized is that people just want to steal things from you.

Mike O'Meara

You have to sell everything for a dollar, because that's all people are going to pay for anything. It doesn't matter what it is. It could be a brick of gold, and people will only pay a fucking dollar for it.

And incidentally, old white ladies don't even want to pay that. What old white ladies want is for you to die so that they can go into your house and find the most expensive antique and take it in their little talons and put it in the back of their Cadillac and take it home.

They come in very briefly to survey the area, like an osprey would survey a flattened lake bed to find the shallow areas where the best fish are. They float above the yard sale, looking down their hawked noses to see if they can find something they can steal from you. If they find a particular glass bowl that Louis XIV took a pee in at some point and buy it for a dollar, their decade is made.

Robb Spewak

There are so many great dynamics happening on that show. For example, me telling Mike over and over again that his stuff is tantamount to worthless. I don't think any other show is doing that, and not only did we do it, but all of us together turned it into something fun.

That show would never have aired on modern radio. We'd have gotten called into a program director's office if we did that. As a podcast, however, we are not constrained. We can be as goofy as we want, and I really love that.

Carla O'Meara

The yard sale show was fun. I learned a lot about pricing, so I didn't need Robb's help any more after that.

Robb Spewak

There was no second yard sale show. I was no longer needed. It broke my heart.

TMOS and Terrestrial Radio

Mike O'Meara

It would have to be an amazing circumstance to get me back on the radio in a traditional sense. We've got a fantastic partner in KCJJ, but do we want to expand into additional stations? You never say never, but I really enjoy what I'm doing right now. We've made it as easy as possible for stations to pick up the show; we've formatted the podcast for radio. However, I'd much rather cater to my podcast audience than a program director, so if a podcast is all we will ever be, I am happy with that. If we are able to feed our families this way, that's fine.

Radio has been very, very good to me over the years, but radio has also kicked me squarely in the balls. I've given a lot of my life to radio, and it's also bitten me in the ass a few times. That happens once, you say, "It's been a good run." It happens twice within a couple of years, and you've had enough. Radio is just like a lot of media in America right now, dictated by a bunch of scared rabbits that get nervous around innovative, original content. I am not really anxious to jump back into an environment where people are playing scared.

I want the creative freedom to do new and exciting things for our listeners. Because I am not constrained by radio management, I don't have to run anything up the flagpole. If we get a stupid, wonderful, beautiful idea from *anybody*, we can make it happen. That's not as easy to do in radio.

Podcasting, the new media, is where we are, knee-deep and getting deeper all the time. This is where the talent is now. This is where the creativity lives. Podcasts are where you can hear some real, cutting-edge, unique stuff, and I am lucky as hell to be a part of it.

7

A DAY THAT WILL LIVE
IN INFAMY

Once the non-compete clause of Mike's contract had expired, he was free to pursue new broadcasting opportunities. On a whim, at the urging of Oscar, Mike gave podcasting a try. *The Mike O'Meara Show* podcast debuted on December 7, 2009, the anniversary of the 1941 Pearl Harbor attack that drew the United States into World War II. Roosevelt described that December 7th as "a day that would live in infamy," because the U.S. had been fundamentally altered by a single event. So, too, the landscape of *TMOS* changed on a December 7th, though the foreign policy implications were far less severe. In this chapter, we revisit the humble beginnings of the *TMOS* podcast, from inspiration to the first broadcast.

Resurrecting TMOS

Oscar Santana

Resurrecting *The Mike O'Meara Show* as a podcast was my idea. I called Mike multiple times. I stalked him. I mentioned it to Mike as he was leaving the radio station for the last time, and Mike didn't bat an eye. I could tell Mike wasn't listening to me because he gave me the "Yeah, yeah, yeah, yeah, yeah" and kept walking. I understood what he was feeling, because he was in the middle of getting his ass canned publically for the first time. I'd lost so many radio station jobs that I was more used to this kind of transition than Mike was.

After a few weeks, I called Mike to talk about it, just to check in and see how he was doing. He was riding out the non-compete clause from his WJFK contract, so there was nothing he could do at the moment. Then he got married and had an "I married Carla" party. I was there and I mentioned the podcast idea to Mike again. He said, "Yeah, I need to talk to my agent." He still wasn't interested.

Finally, as his contract was expiring, Mike called me and asked, "What's a podcast?" as if I hadn't explained it to him a hundred times already.

He hadn't been listening to me at all, but I really don't blame him. You're Mike O'Meara and you've just been part of a format flip. You're waiting for that phone to ring, and why wouldn't it? But I had seen all these big-name radio talents who had been let go and weren't getting hired—radio had changed and no one was looking to pick up talent with a big salary.

Mike O'Meara
The idea of being an Internet entity was strange. I was always thinking about getting back on the radio. Podcasting was not on my radar.

Oscar Santana
TMOS is a brand, and by dropping them CBS basically said, "We have no interest in selling this incredible brand because it's not our area of focus anymore." And they let it go. People were already podcasting, and as smart phones got more

popular, I knew people would love access to their favorite shows on demand, any time they wanted.

The first time I ever did a podcast was in 2005. I remember going to my program director and asking if I could make *Big O and Dukes* available as a podcast. She looked at me like I was an alien, but we did it anyway. I think we were the first radio talk show, at that point, that also had a podcast on iTunes. By the time *TMOS* ended its terrestrial radio run in 2009, I had been podcasting for four years.

Tony Perkins

Because of the time period that Mike and I grew up in, broadcasting was the thing. That was it. In fact, even when cable came along, I was thinking, "Yeah, I'm not doing *cable*." Obviously cable is huge now, but when I think of broadcasting, I still think of television and radio. I'm kind of a dinosaur that way.

Mike O'Meara

Initially, I had no interest in doing a podcast. To me, a podcaster was a guy who lived in his mother's house and had a computer in his basement. Not for me. No thanks.

Oscar Santana

When Mike O'Meara finally called me, I explained to him that he's a brand, one that a big communications company foolishly undervalued. I told him that he should start podcasting his show, because there was an audience that would keep listening to and looking for him. The longer he stayed off the air in one form or another, the harder it was for them to find him.

I said, "Let's talk about this, but remember that I have a 9-to-5 marketing job now in Manassas." Coincidentally, Mike lived in Manassas. I said, "Let's meet at the Uno's Pizzeria up the street."

He showed up with his wife around 6:30 p.m. I explained to him what I thought was possible for him and his show. I had no aspirations of actually being a cohost—I was going to help on the business side if they needed it. He was interested enough to agree to another meeting with the other guys, Robb and Buzz.

Robb Spewak

I think it was probably about a month and a half after the layoff that Oscar brought me into the conversation, talking about going into another medium. A "podcast," a thing I did not understand. I remember a lunch with Oscar, Mike, Buzz, and me, with Oscar trying to explain everything.

Oscar Santana

I explained my vision to them, a condensed show that would be broadcast online, on-demand.

Robb Spewak

We used to do four hours a day, so the thought of just doing an hour or so did not feel like enough. He asked me, "Do you think in your wildest dreams that anyone listened to all four hours of your radio show?" I said, "Frankly, Oscar, I didn't even listen to all four hours."

He said, "The reason you do four hours is because you're broadcasting on the radio, so you provide a larger window for people to jump in and drop out. If someone listens to you an hour a day on the radio, you are fantastic—you are Michael Jordan. When you broadcast a condensed version, you give them their hour that they can fit into their schedule. Whenever they want to grab their hour, it's going to be there. And that's how this works."

Mike O'Meara

Right away, I loved the idea of a condensed broadcast, a concentrated version of what I had done on the radio for years and years. It was all the good stuff, the very best of what we do, and there was a more relaxed feeling because you didn't have that pressure of having to fill four or five hours a day.

Robb Spewak

The show is exactly 79 minutes long, and unlike the four-hour broadcast we used to do, people are actually listening to all 79 minutes of us every day.

Mike O'Meara

I also liked that podcast listeners had to be active listeners. People are actively downloading our shows—going out and grabbing them. It's just you and the listener, and that's it. There's no middle man, no program director analyzing every word.

Most radio stations are a bunch of middle men and that's what has helped to ruin radio. There are too many middle men, too many filters. In the land of podcasting you don't have those filters. You know what your audience wants because they tell you, and you deliver it.

Oscar Santana

They looked at me, especially Robb and Buzz, like I was crazy when they heard my pitch. At the end of that meeting, I think they were thinking, "Why the hell not? This will last for two weeks, but I guess it's all we've got—there's nothing else going on, so this will kill some time." That's the vibe I got.

Tony Perkins

When I first heard Mike was going to do a podcast, I thought, "Oh, wow. That is ... too bad."

Mary O'Meara

I know nothing about podcasts, so I don't even know what Mike is doing. I always hoped Mike would grow up to be Walter Cronkite, but that didn't materialize. At 93, I don't want a computer, because I'm not coming into this century.

Leap of Faith

Oscar Santana

Next thing you know, Mike and I are at Guitar Center purchasing all the equipment for the studio.

Robb Spewak

It didn't take long to build the living room studio and get it sounding the way we wanted it to. In time, we got the studio sounding better than we ever did on the air. We had better equipment than the radio station!

Oscar Santana

While we were at Guitar Center, Mike asked me, "Would you like to sit in with us?" I asked him what he meant, figuring he was asking me to come on as a guest for the first show when everything was set up and they were ready to broadcast.

He said, "I mean do you want to be part of the show? It was your idea. You should be on the show and we can do this together. You did five hours of radio a day. Five hours! I did four, you did five and in mid-days of all places. You should come and work with us."

Mike O'Meara

I thought it might be cool to take in the orphan and put him on my show. I'd always gotten along with Big O and Dukes. I liked Oscar's energy and style, so I knew that bringing him on-board would enhance the product.

Oscar Santana

I told Mike I'd love to join the show, but under one condition. I said, "Let's give it a couple of weeks, and if my presence on the show is like forcing a square peg into a round hole, let's be straight and honest with each other. I don't want to detract from what you, Robb, and Buzz have done over the last 25 years. If I don't fit, I don't want to stay and ruin *TMOS*."

Robb Spewak

Once, Steve Bridges flew me out to Iowa to promote KCJJ and to do my music show live during the downtime, before the podcast. Over dinner, he asked what *else* we had planned. I told him we were going to do something called a podcast and that he couldn't tell anybody because it was secret.

He said, "I won't tell anybody. But I want it." I told him we didn't even have it yet or quite know what *it* is. He said, "Whatever it is, I want it."

I asked, "Steve, do you know what a tremendous, reverse technology guy you are?" He asked me what I meant. I said, "It's taken about 80 years of radio for broadcasting to develop into podcasting, and in one week you've put it back on AM radio. You've taken a tremendous step backwards for everybody."

Steve Bridges

Mike has been a part of my radio station for over 18 years. I didn't like the period of time between the end of *TMOS* and the beginning of the podcast. I didn't like that Mike wasn't a part of the station. We had Robb, but we really missed the other guys. When they said they were going to do a podcast, I said, "I want it. I want to carry that, whatever it is."

Kappy Pfeiffer

When it was clear that *TMOS* was going to start this podcast, I knew they would need capital. I approached them and said, "Once advertisers and sponsors start coming in and you find premium products, you'll be flying. Until then, you need money." That seemed to come at a really good time for them, and thank goodness. Seriously, I would hate to be without their show. This was the first time I did something like this, and it was very exciting.

When I started approaching the show to offer investment capital, I knew Mike and the guys to some degree on Facebook. I gave them the money anonymously, under a fake name. I had my accountant send them checks that didn't identify me. I had begun a Facebook friendship with them, and I didn't want to tarnish that with talk about money.

Episode One

Oscar Santana

Once we were set up and ready to record the first podcast, I was really nervous. It wasn't just a vision or a concept I was selling anymore—everything was coming to fruition. We were putting real dollars, real time into this project. Mike, Robb, and Buzz, three guys I really respect, were following my game plan. They were spending their time and money to do this, and I was hoping it wasn't a waste of their time.

If we built it, would they come? We hadn't even done a full show when we sat down to record the first episode. We ran a few sound checks to tune the equipment, but that was it.

I got even more nervous when we started the show and Mike went right to the negative, telling people, "I'm not one of you!" He's yelling it from the top of Mount Rushmore. I was thinking, "Oh, no! What are you doing? You're alienating all these people on the Internet!" No one would invite you over to his house and then the first thing that comes out of his mouth is, "I'm not one of you!" Who does that?

But then you realize he's not talking to you, the listener. He's talking to all the other guys in the business with a microphone, a board, and Adobe Audition software. He's right. He's not Internet Radio Tommy. He's Mike Fucking O'Meara.

TMOS Episode #1, Recorded December 7, 2009
The Mike O'Meara Show Returns

Mike O'Meara

I want to make this point. There are Internet radio shows out there, and I don't want to sound like an egomaniacal bastard, but I'm going to sound like an egomaniacal bastard, okay? This goes out to all of my "brethren" in the Internet radio biz: I'M NOT ONE OF YOU! I'M NOT F-ING ONE OF YOU HACKS!

I'm not part of your family. I am a disc jockey who was on the air for 25 plus years who got S-canned. I am not somebody who sold his mother's car to pretend that I am a disc jockey. It pisses me off that I have gotten emails that say, "Hey, welcome to Internet radio."

Oscar Santana

Just so I'm clear, you're not one of them?

Mike O'Meara

I'm not one of them. This is a broadcast radio program, by professionals, that is going out over the Internet. I've wanted to get this off my chest for a long time.

I get these emails, "Come on ZZBZ radio and join Zippy and the Zipperhead for a nice little conversation. We're going to be down at Hoochie's Taco House on Saturday and we're bringing our station wagon so we can do our show down there."

Oscar Santana

While you say you're not one of them, they broadcast from somewhere in their home and we happen to be in your living room. They usually don't get paid, and we're not getting paid.

Mike O'Meara

Not yet, damn it.

Oscar Santana

They hope for some sort of "traction" on their shows, and so do we. Finally, they bought their gear at Guitar Center ...

Mike O'Meara

Don't mention that! We haven't gotten a dime off of them!

Robb Spewak

But do the other guys have special curtains? ▪

———

Oscar Santana

Once the show was over, I sat there wondering what the download numbers were going to look like. It didn't take long to find out: the numbers were massive, more than I ever dreamed. I remember watching that ticker, like sitting by a microwave waiting for my food to cook.

I watched it count up: 5,000 within an hour; 10,000 within two hours. Holy shit! We hit 15,000 three hours after the show went live and ended up with almost 50,000 downloads on that first day. An arena of listeners downloaded us. We could have filled up the Verizon Center more than two times over.

In one day we went from four unemployed guys—I was technically employed in the technology field but I wanted to be in radio—to four guys who realized they could make this podcast work and earn a living doing it.

Carla O'Meara

I remember Mike saying, "Oh my gosh, Carla, people are actually listening."

Robb Spewak

So many people tried to download the first show that it crashed our server. We may have had even more than 50,000 if not for that. I remember Oscar telling me the show was down because of the crash, and my initial thought was, "Oh, great, of course that would happen. But then my second thought was, "Oh, GREAT. Listeners care *that much*. There is an urgency to listen."

If we had to have one screw up to start the first show, that was a great one. There was such a demand for *TMOS* that it caused trouble, and I would rather have that than an error-free upload to an audience of 80 people. The show has only grown since.

Oscar Santana

I am proud to have been part of the creation and resurrection of *TMOS*. I'm happy that I wasn't too scared to call Mike and say, "I think we can do this. I know we can do this."

Tony Perkins

I have the utmost respect for what Mike is doing. It's right in line with the times and with technology. It will be a different kind of success than Mike is used to, different than having a nationally-syndicated radio show, different from being the top-rated show in the market for his time slot. But it is still success nonetheless. We're all having to get used to success being defined differently.

Living on the Edge

While the podcast served to scratch Mike's broadcasting itch, he longed to return to terrestrial radio. Less than a year after the podcast began, he was back on the air, partnered with Kirk McEwen at 105.9 The Edge FM in Washington, D.C. Over the 14-month life of that program, which ended with another station flip, O'Meara truly began to lament the business and politics of radio. The podcast was no longer an experiment. It became his lifeline.

Mike O'Meara

I got a call from Jeff Bowden, who was the head of the Citadel cluster in Washington, D.C., a day or two after I had been laid off from WJFK. We had a long conversation, but I waited about a year to have my agent contact Citadel to try and work something out.

Kenny King, the program director at The Edge, and I had been in contact, and he eventually asked me if I would come back on the air. I really wanted to bring my whole show, my whole team, over to 105.9 and, unfortunately, it didn't work out. At that point, I really wanted to be back on the radio—that's all I had known for many years and it's how I defined success. I told Kenny if coming back alone was my only choice, I'd do it.

They eventually decided to partner me with a guy of their choosing, Kirk McEwen. He'd been on the station already and was a known commodity. Plus he had done morning radio before.

When the radio opportunity arose for me alone, I wanted to make sure that the guys who had started this podcast with me were still going to be able to feed their families. There was never any question: I was going to keep doing the podcast in addition to the morning radio show on The Edge. My contract even stipulated that I could continue doing the podcast.

It was a tough year, getting up at 4:00 a.m. to do a 5:30–9:00 morning show every day and then coming back home at 11:00 a.m. to do the podcast. When I got hired at The Edge, radio was still reeling from the recession, so it was frustrating. There was so much turmoil and everyone was unsettled. They all wondered if their station was next to go.

The radio station had previous format changes and it didn't have a lot of traction going in, including no previous morning show. I always thought that we should have had some sort of rollout for *The Kirk and Mike Show*, but it happened really fast. I think I was offered the job on a Wednesday and started the following Monday.

In my zeal to get back on the radio, I'd jumped into another horseshit radio situation with scared management. It was my toughest year on the podcast. Returning to terrestrial radio was not what I had expected it would be and I was not happy there. That made me difficult to live with, here at home, on the podcast, and probably for my radio partners Kirk and Shamrock on The Edge.

One good thing came of my time on The Edge, though. I learned how much more I loved doing the podcast than being on the air. The podcast became my landing spot, my passion. Yes, the podcast was broadcast from my home, but doing the podcast began to feel like home for me.

8

LIVE FROM HIS COUCH

Now that *TMOS* has broadcast over 1,000 regular episodes and hundreds of additional bonus and special episodes, it is hard to imagine a time when the viability of the podcast as a business venture was ever in doubt. The podcast has some obvious differences from its radio ancestry, including running time and broadcast location, but these have not handicapped its success. Neither have the less obvious changes in the show, including the lack of a radio sales staff, large advertising budgets, and free access to powerful broadcasting equipment.

There is no secret sauce in the *TMOS* recipe; the key ingredients have always been the hosts and the chemistry they share. Their ability to generate compelling content powers the show, whether it originates from a radio studio or an overstuffed sofa in the O'Meara living room.

While radio was adamant that it didn't need talk shows like *TMOS* to succeed, the reverse turned out to be true. Talk shows like *TMOS* had no need of radio.

The New Normal

Mike O'Meara

My greatest professional satisfaction used to come from being rated number one in a specific demographic or getting a bonus. It took a while to understand just how wrong that perspective was. Now my personal satisfaction comes from the feedback I get from my listening audience.

It's a different kind of show when you do 79 minutes versus 4 hours. When you have to fill a lot of time, you resort to interviews, contesting, and taking phone calls. There are times when I miss some of that stuff, but I prefer the show the way it is now.

Arch Campbell

I first met Mike in the 1980s when he was part of *The Don and Mike Show* on WAVA 105.1 FM. They invited me over to their studios a couple of times. I remember the first visit very clearly. When I walked into the studio, there was a rather large woman in there, who despite not being very attractive was wearing no clothes at all. Nothing.

They were doing a segment called Strip Trivia where listeners would come in on their way to work in the morning and answer trivia questions. When they got questions wrong, they'd take off their clothes right there in front of everyone.

At that time I was working with Channel 4 television news, and back then television was a fairly conservative medium. I thought to myself, "This is it. My career is over. I am on the air with naked people."

Then I noticed it was not just one naked listener in there but three. There were also two young people, a man and a woman in their 20s, and they were also naked. The girl was hot, just beautiful. Here's this gorgeous young woman, who stopped by *The Don and Mike Show* to take her clothes off for them, and they're not even looking at her—they don't even acknowledge that she's completely naked right in front of them.

Mike O'Meara

Strip Trivia was one thing you could do on the radio that would get a lot of attention and also fill a lot of time. It's not something I'd do in my living room, though. I have a feeling Carla might have a problem with that.

Mike Kelley

I get a more positive vibe from *TMOS* than I did from the old *Don and Mike Show*. Would you agree?

Robb Spewak

I would agree that we have a slightly more positive energy now. This coming from Mike and I, who are two of the most negative men in the world. We can really turn sunshine into a sunburn just like *that*, but I do think the show is more light-hearted. There are more laughs to be had. There were people who, in other incarnations of the show, really did love the negativity. They all lived in Sacramento, California.

———

Mike O'Meara

After 25–30 years in radio, you tune in to what people want to hear. You don't have to rely on hacky DJ prep services to send you discussion topics or sit there with the newspaper to find things to talk about. All shows are going to discuss the hot current events of the day, but that can't be all you talk about.

Listeners love to hear personal stories, especially if they're self-deprecating. That's what people want. That's what's ultimately compelling. If you take that away, if we're just talking about Kim Kardashian every day, you're not going to have a show. My listeners are much more interested in something that happened to Robb, Oscar, or me than they are the standard generic talk show topics.

Robb Spewak

We've got the same 20 news items from the Associated Press that every other talk show has, but it's our spin on them that makes them unique. It's like *Iron Chef*. We've got the same ingredients as everyone else, but we're going to make the best tasting food.

Mike O'Meara

You have to watch for the little things that happen to you every day—things you might take for granted that could result in phenomenal material and turn into something very special.

Catherine O'Meara

Every single time we say something funny, my dad says, "Using that for the show, using that for the show."

Elizabeth O'Meara

He carries around a yellow note pad and writes notes to himself all the time.

Mike O'Meara

The best content for our show would be if one of us was an eyewitness to a disaster that was somehow funny. Let me create a hypothetical for you, the greatest situation: Robb gets trapped at the top of a roller coaster.

Oscar Santana

That would be fantastic.

Mike O'Meara

Wouldn't that be special? I almost want to pay someone to make it happen. We wouldn't want anyone to be killed.

Robb Spewak

No, of course not.

Mike O'Meara

Maimed, maybe.

Robb Spewak

You want stories about danger? You want danger? I'm your man.

Mike O'Meara

Show preparation requires a dedication, a commitment. Even with solid prep, you still have to be ready to dance when that microphone's on. As Don and I used to say on a regular basis, "Be ready to make pudding out of shit." That's an art form, and in my case, it takes a lifetime to learn.

This is the advice I would give baby broadcasters. You should focus on what you like, what your real interests are, and don't fake it. Then you have to find out what is uniquely yours and try to make that interesting to the listeners.

Legendary TMOS Stories

When the personal stories of its hosts compose the most memorable moments on the show, some of those stories are bound to be, shall we say, less than flattering. I asked Mike, Robb, and Oscar to recount their most embarrassing personal stories that became part of the *TMOS* canon.

Mike O'Meara

Once when I was between marriages, I was dating a woman who happened to be a police officer. I had just gotten out of one relationship and I'd finally found another woman. I was dating, it was regular, and it was fun.

This young lady and I had planned to go to Bermuda together. The arrangement was that she would arrive at my house on a Friday afternoon and we would fly down to Bermuda early Saturday morning. She'd spend the night at my house. She got to my house at roughly 3:00 a.m. Saturday and I was pissed. I felt like she had been out with somebody else; I felt like this was not starting the trip the right way. I continued to be pissed.

I had no problem expressing my displeasure to her, and even with that, we still gave it a go and got on the plane to Bermuda. As we got down there, it became more and more evident that she was pissed at me and I was pissed at her. We went back and forth, and ultimately I made a comment about her mother—that she might have preferred the company of other women. It was not my best moment.

Robb Spewak

You made an implication.

Mike O'Meara

I did so in a very harsh way that I am not proud of.

Oscar Santana

You jerk.

Mike O'Meara

I made the comment when I realized all was lost, that she was done with me. I was going to say the meanest thing I possibly could. Something that I highly recommend people do in all healthy relationships.

That is when she decided that she was going to be leaving the following day, and not only that but she was moving into another room in the hotel where we were staying. So, I decided to take a little two-wheel scooter into the town of Hamilton, Bermuda to drown my sorrows. Boy, am I good at that. To make a long story short, I drank for most of the day there and into the wee the hours of the morning. I ended up at an exclusively local Bermuda nightclub where I believe I was the only person of Irish-American extraction.

I remember that I had, late at night, given some guy money to go make a phone call and he vanished. I staggered out onto the street. At that point, there was a guy who asked me for my wallet, in a rather threatening way. Because I was drowning my sorrows and not feeling particularly positive about life in general, I challenged him to a fight. He reached into a trash barrel and pulled out a broken bottle. I still continued to advance on him.

Robb Spewak
The irony? Mike was responsible for emptying the bottle.

Mike O'Meara
When he looked at me, my expression must have indicated my desperate state, that I didn't give a shit if I was killed at that point. He turned tail and ran. That's how low I was. I was terrifying thieves.

I continued to make bad decisions throughout the night, including climbing back onto the scooter at 6:30 a.m. As I wobbled my way back to the hotel, I decided it would be a fantastic idea to go see the young lady who was, at that moment, going to the airport to be rid of me.

Oscar Santana
Oh, God.

Mike O'Meara

Although I knew there was nothing I could say to make her stay, I just wanted to chalk this up to a bad experience. Her comment, I believe, was "You're a wonderful guy, but you've got some anger issues."

At that point, she reached into her purse and said, "By the way, here's your passport." She was planning to get on the plane with my passport, stranding me there out of spite. I said goodbye, got back on my scooter, returned to the hotel, cracked open an Amstel Light at 7:00 a.m., and watched her plane fly off to Washington, D.C.

Many of my listeners will already know that story. My pain delighted many people, and it helped me purge by sharing it.

Robb Spewak

It's a legendary story.

Mike O'Meara

It's therapy. My second most embarrassing story was the Bulldog story.

Robb Spewak

Please don't hurry through this.

Mike O'Meara

It was during *The Don and Mike Show*. Our producer was Frank Murphy and the assistant producer was Diana Silman. I had given Diana a gag birthday gift called the Bulldog, this giant dildo that was a recreation of a massive, veiny penis. There was much laughter and mirth over the gift.

Flash forward a few weeks. I had a recording session for some commercial work up in Columbia, Maryland, and I was driving from Arlington, Virginia. It takes about an hour depending on traffic. At that time, Don and I were very successful on WAVA, enjoying tremendous ratings. I got into my car, an Acura Legend.

Robb Spewak

They named it after you!

Mike O'Meara

It was a little two-door coupe with a grill on the front. I headed on my way, super morning DJ going to do his super voice work for his super commercial. Super duper. Right away, someone hit the horn when I pulled onto the road. They gave me a thumbs-up. I winked and pointed at them, the Superstar. This happened not once, not twice, but three times before I even got to the main highway.

Robb Spewak

When you receive that kind of unsolicited recognition, what are you thinking?

Mike O'Meara

I am thinking, "How hot are we? This is awesome! Everybody is listening to *The Don and Mike Show*, and people are recognizing me because of my TV commercials. I am hot! Mr. Big Shot." This happens maybe seven or eight times on the trip. I get waved at on the Beltway. I get waved at on Route 66. I get pointed to on Route 29.

Oscar Santana

You're steering with your raging erection at this point.

Mike O'Meara

I get up to where the recording studio is and backed the car into a spot in front of a big glass window. There are people waiting in line who turn around and smile at me.

Robb Spewak

You're on fire!

Mike O'Meara

"Everybody knows me," I am thinking. I winked and went in to do my recording session for about two hours. I come out, walk to the front of my car, and there, wedged into the front grill of my Acura Legend, is a giant, flesh-colored, 8-inch, veiny penis. Frank and Diana had wedged this thing into the grill of my car.

Robb Spewak

Hours ago!

Mike O'Meara

I suddenly realized that everybody wasn't pointing and waving at the radio superstar. They were pointing and waving at the stupid ass with the dildo sticking out of his car. I had the wonderful exercise of trying to dislodge this member from the front of my Acura Legend.

Robb Spewak

Please tell me there's surveillance camera footage of that.

Mike O'Meara

When I finally realized the joke was on me, I was hoping to tug it out, but it required a lot of leverage. It was really wedged in there. It took two hands and a lot of prying. They didn't want that thing to go flying out of the grill.

Robb Spewak

Of course! When you mount a dildo to a motor vehicle, your primary concern must be for the safety of others, Mike.

———

Robb Spewak

The memory of our listeners is always remarkable to me, especially when it relates to their memory of my mistakes. Three or four times a year, a specific story comes up that I hate, because the only villain in it is me. It makes me look like a total tool.

It was Christmas, and it was the worst Christmas Cary and I ever had together. The kids did okay, because they were younger and kids at Christmas are pretty much fine. For your wife, you always try to have one cornerstone gift that's going to tell her she's a great wife. She looks at you and says you're a great husband.

I remembered her saying to me that she wanted a piece of jewelry, something specific: a white gold cross necklace. Something simple, something understated. I went and found a really nice one, paid retail. Didn't even trade it out—paid full price.

Oscar Santana
True love.

Robb Spewak
Also there was no trade to be had. I bought it, wrapped it, did the whole thing where you put it way behind the tree so it's the last thing she opens. She opened it and her face fell. I said, "You don't like it." She said, "Oh, it's beautiful." I said, "It's exactly what you asked for." She said, "Yes. It's exactly what you bought me last Christmas."

Oscar Santana
You're such an asshole.

Robb Spewak
She had requested a white gold cross about 19 months earlier, and I bought it for her Christmas 2004 *and* Christmas 2005. It escalated into yelling. She had to do something with the kids the day after Christmas. I took down the tree, put away all the decorations, returned her cross, and she came home that afternoon and said, "It's like Christmas never happened." I said to her, "If only that were true."

Mike Kelley

We call that the Christmas double-cross.

Robb Spewak

Exactly! You feel like such a total ass, but as Mike said, when you purge it all on the air, it takes away some of the sting. I'd say it's about every three months that I do something stupid, maritally-speaking, and someone puts a picture of a white gold cross on my Facebook page.

Mike O'Meara

And that story is a prime example of why we call Robb a great listener.

Robb Spewak

Hey, I listened! I just didn't remember buying it.

———

Oscar Santana

I think the most embarrassing thing for me goes back to my conflict resolution in a failed relationship. The way that I basically fought in what I thought was a methodical way was actually ... well, no one wins in that situation.

Mike O'Meara

The story of the destroyed property.

Robb Spewak

To be fair, he started small, by breaking her sunglasses.

Oscar Santana

I was in a horrible relationship and things were getting shady. She was having late night phone conversations and sudden "I have to work tonight" situations. At this point in my life, I had just switched careers into the business world and started with *The Mike O'Meara Show*. I didn't have a lot of extra time for a relationship. I own that, but it all came to a head in the Halloween of 2011.

I went out that night with my girl, came home hammered, woke up around 3 a.m. with my Super Mario costume on that I had passed out in. I heard her speaking to someone out in front of the condo complex. The building was mostly empty because they were remodeling the place, so the sound carried more than normal.

Mike O'Meara
You overheard her having a phone conversation.

Oscar Santana
I couldn't quite make it out. I was disheveled with my Mario mustache stuck in my ear. I opened the front door, asked what she was doing on the phone at that hour, and asked who she was secretly talking to.

She told me she was talking to her sister's boyfriend—something weird, something that didn't make sense. I knew she had been lying, and instead of raging out about it and going crazy, I told her it didn't add up. Keep in mind I had been drinking, so that complicates any attempt at conflict resolution.

Robb Spewak
And besides, you're wearing oversized Mario overalls.

Oscar Santana
I asked to see her phone to investigate the truth, but she had erased the call records. I asked why she'd do that, and I asked if we could go online to see if we could look up who she was talking to. She told me she didn't have her password.

Robb Spewak
A series of miscommunications.

Oscar Santana
I should have stopped right there and walked away, but Hammered Mario was still playing Nancy Drew. I picked

127

up the first thing in front of me, some wonderful sunglasses that were too expensive that I'd bought for her. In the corner of my eye, I saw a MacBook Pro and an iPod Touch which I had also bought for my girlfriend. I couldn't afford any of them, but I was so thankful we had gotten through the layoff, a rough patch in my career. I was happy that we were coming out on top.

Now it was 4 a.m. I said, "I am going to give you 15 minutes to tell me the truth, to show me some sort of phone records to straighten this out. Every 15 minutes, I will break something of yours I bought you."

Mike O'Meara

If I remember this story correctly, Oscar had a little difficulty understanding that was still an abusive action.

Oscar Santana

I still don't think it's abuse. I'm going on record.

Mike O'Meara

Well, put it in print. Send the letters to Oscar Santana.

Oscar Santana

It wasn't the best way to resolve a conflict. There was no resolution. After 15 minutes I broke the sunglasses. It's not like I threw them at her. I did it in a controlled environment—in my hands.

Robb Spewak

And just like a true disc jockey, always by the clock. He's breaking them on the quarters and then on the 8s he gave traffic.

Oscar Santana

Fifteen minutes later, I broke the iPod. I did that outside so I wouldn't get glass in the condo. The laptop got broken at the top of the hour. That sucked. Looking back now, it was my lowest moment. Not just as a human being, I would say, but as a broadcaster when I told the story later on the air. I was ashamed, but sometimes you just have to purge and tell the truth.

Mike O'Meara

Oscar's extremely well-regarded for sharing that story. He's complimented about it on Facebook.

Oscar Santana

I delete those posts.

Robb Spewak

And then he breaks their Facebook accounts.

Oscar Santana

Another lowlight involves Mentisan. It's like a menthol Vaseline rub, but it's made in Bolivia. When I was 30 and living at home ...

Robb Spewak

I always found it entertaining when you called your parents your "roommates."

Oscar Santana

So my roommate, my mom, saw I had the flu. You know when you're sick on the radio it sucks. You still have to go in and be the hero. My mom said, "Do you want me to put Mentisan on you?"

I was talking about this on *Big O and Dukes*, explaining that it's a home remedy no one knows about, this secret witchcraft remedy that was going to blow everyone's socks off.

Mike O'Meara

So when you were a kid, your mom would rub Mentisan on your chest.

Oscar Santana

When I had the flu and I was 30, I was still staying in my childhood bedroom. I told my radio partner Chad that my mom came in my room and started rubbing Mentisan on my chest like she would when I was younger. So here's another wrinkle. When I was in college, my mom would help me wax my chest.

Mike O'Meara

Oh my God.

Oscar Santana

My mom mentioned, as she was rubbing my chest, "You might need a wax sometime soon."

Robb Spewak

How do you spell "Mentisan"? Is it O-E-D-I-P-U-S?

Oscar Santana

I thought I was going to be a folk remedy hero and all I did was make everything weird. Everyone in the room heard how weird it was but me. I had to field an onslaught of calls, all these people telling me that I needed therapy. Naked cruelty.

Robb Spewak

Literally!

9

LIFE IN THE PUBLIC EYE

Perhaps the greatest failing of the Internet in modern society is its tacit reassurance that everyone's opinions are important. If you ever want to lose faith in humanity, spend time trudging through public comments on the web for any news article or YouTube® video. Searching for a well-written, carefully considered comment is like panning for gold in cow manure—not only is it a waste of time, but when you're done, you feel filthy all over.

Before you climb onto a high horse, though, think for a moment about how hasty you are to pronounce your own judgments. I boggle at the number of times I have watched a television show, turned to my wife, and said, "I hate that guy." I make this comment off the cuff, casually. Somehow, because a random actor trying to earn a living has not entertained me for a millisecond, I have decided that he has earned my disdain. As much as I'd like to point fingers at the sneerers, the naysayers, the snarky know-it-alls, I too often find myself engaging in the same behavior. I don't think about what it feels like to be the target of such abject judgment.

Many people dream of fame and fortune, but they forget the flip side of the celebrity coin. For some reason, "Do unto others as you would have them do unto you" goes out the window when the "others" live public lives. The hosts of *TMOS* share personal stories and open themselves up to their listeners, living life in the public eye. I asked each of them to help me understand what it is like to be under scrutiny every day, to know that no matter what you do or say, people are continually passing judgment on you. Is it honestly even worth the trouble?

Precarious Privacy

Robb Spewak

One of the best things about spending so much time on the air is the sheer volume of footage about my family. My parents have a total of, between them, 25 or 30 seconds of silent, Super 8 film of them as kids. That and some photographs. That's it.

Since I was 21 years old, there are hours and hours and *hours* of my life captured and saved, not just by me but by listeners and under-the-radar websites. I've got long segments of my kids when they were very little coming on the radio. I love hearing the audio of my kids—I think it's purer than video. A kid on videotape tends to know he's being videotaped, but audio recordings are different. Kids aren't as guarded. I go back to audio tapes of my kids much more often than I do videos of them.

There are pieces of tape when I announced I was going to be married and others when I told everyone I was going to have a baby. That's a pretty powerful time capsule, and it's a privilege not many people have.

Oscar Santana

My greatest fear is that my mom suddenly likes talk radio. It's not like I talk about anything embarrassing or disrespectful about my friends and family on the air, except ... wait ... that's exactly what I do every day.

Because I talk about so much about my personal life, my girlfriend Shannon had to stop listening. She loves the show—she loved it before we were even dating—so it wasn't an easy choice for her, but it made things easier for both of us. No one in my life had ever listened to my shows, but she used to. It was really cool. I would come home and she'd talk to me about them, telling me what she thought was funny. It's almost like having a small focus group, one that supports you. But when we got into our first couple of arguments and I talked about them on the air, she didn't like that. I don't blame her. It has to be different for her as an "unwilling participant" on the show she listens to.

In their defense, the people we love don't have an opportunity to get on the air and rebut the things we say. Our stories are one-sided. However, this is really what I do for a living. I am not going to lie to Shannon, telling her I would never talk about our personal lives again. This is my life—it's what I do. It's probably best for us if she stops listening to the shows.

So when she burns the floor, or buys too many plants, or crashes the car, I am free to talk about it, because I know she won't hear me. I don't want to feel like I could get in trouble for saying something on the air when I come home. We're both much happier, personally, since she stopped listening.

Carla O'Meara

Mike's always protected me, and I know he's careful not to make me look bad on the air. I trust him, so I know that whatever he says on the podcast is something we'll both think is funny. I don't know how I'd feel if he told people the bad stuff. I probably wouldn't like it very much.

Catherine O'Meara

My dad is very protective of our privacy. He doesn't want us to be an open book to the world. He tries to shelter us from it, for the most part.

Elizabeth O'Meara

He really does a great job with that. I mean, we never get anything creepy from any of the fans. He does a really good job of making sure to protect us and our private, personal lives.

Sometimes it's tricky because we'll be out with Dad and people recognize him. It seems to happen a lot more, recently, since the podcast started. When we go to Capitals games, he gets recognized at least five times.

Catherine O'Meara

For some reason, at Capitals games, I don't know if it's all the same people or what, but there are so many *TMOS* fans there. I can't imagine being really, really famous, because after being with him and having four or five people come up and say, "Hey, I love the show," it's overwhelming for me at least. I'd just want to get away from it.

Elizabeth O'Meara

Once we were at a Capitals game and someone asked me about a recent orchestra concert I had. It was so strange to have a complete stranger know that I recently had an orchestra concert. You'd almost rather people just say, "I love the show," instead of dropping creepy facts about our lives.

Away from Dad, people don't recognize us, but they will sometimes make the connection with the last name, especially teachers at school.

Catherine O'Meara

Every two months or so, someone comes up to one of us and says, "Your last name's O'Meara. Are you one of Mike O'Meara's daughters?" I try to be friendly about it. Then I try to end the conversation as fast as I can.

Sometimes it can be weird. Once, a teacher saw my name in the roll and asked, "Are you Mike O'Meara's daughter?" I said yes. He said, "Oh, we're going to be best friends," and I thought that was weird. In those situations, I try to avoid continued interaction.

Tony Perkins

The vast majority of people who approach me are enthusiastic. I imagine that the people who don't like what you do decide not to come up to you, but the vast majority of people are wonderful.

The only times that it kind of bothers me are when I am with my son, particularly if it's just me and him. Obviously, I am trying to keep an eye on him and engage with him. I don't mind people approaching me, but sometimes people want to monopolize my time there, and I have to shut that down.

Oddly enough, the weirdest experience I've had happened recently. My great uncle died; we were very close. When his funeral was over, I was walking to my car to get into the funeral procession, and someone drove up next to me as I was walking on the sidewalk. The woman recognized me. "I watch you all the time! What are you doing out here?"

I told her I was attending a funeral. She said, "Oh, okay," and then proceeded to tell me about some project she's working on, a script she's writing or something. She even got out of her car and was walking behind me, telling me about it. I turned around and said, "I'm at a funeral, and I have to get in my car so I can join the funeral procession." I said that multiple times during the "conversation." She actually seemed annoyed.

In all my years, that may have been the weirdest encounter. Usually, interactions with fans are great, but every now and again something weird like that happens.

Radio Personality vs. Real-Life Personality

Mike O'Meara

Everyone on the radio exaggerates certain elements of their personalities. That's the way the game works. On the radio, I tend to be a curmudgeon, but that makes the show more fun. If I was trying to be a sweetheart to everybody, it wouldn't make for entertaining radio. When the microphones are on, I'll say things that I probably wouldn't say in a normal social situation.

Away from the microphones in my day-to-day life, I am much quieter. I'm not always "on." When it's just Carla and me, we're quiet; we're mellow. We like to make each other laugh. With that said, if I'm being honest, I do tend to complain. That's the part of me that I'm not proud of. You get that off the mic as well. Believe me. Especially if you cut me off in traffic.

Robb Spewak

On the show, I am a big, bloviating loudmouth. At home, my wife's the boss. After nearly 17 years of marriage, I've figured out what system works for us. I defer to her. She runs our household.

On the show I am loud and brash, often saying things that I think people wish they could say but can't get away with in modern society. In real life, most of the time I'm polite and maybe even, in a totally foreign setting, shy. I am not nearly as extroverted as a lot of people think I am.

I do stuff with other parents and kids, and you can't be a loudmouth like that in real life, lest they label you an asshole. You don't want that. You don't want to be the people that no one wants to associate with because their father is "that disc jockey."

Mike O'Meara

On our show, I can give people every side of me. I can read a letter I've written to my newborn son and get emotional. I can compliment Robb or Oscar. Then, two minutes later, I can tell them to go to hell. I can be a complete and total bastard, or I can be all sweetness and light. Just like in real life.

Carla O'Meara

Mike on the radio is not the real Mike. If I didn't know him and I was only a listener, I wouldn't believe what I am saying right now. I would think, "How could that not be the way he really is?" Off the radio, he is completely the opposite. Mike is very reserved and quiet.

Mike O'Meara

Usually reserved. I have done things on and off the air that I am not proud of. I do not suffer fools, and I hate it when people behave badly. I am usually more reserved off the air, but I have my moments.

Oscar Santana

Although there are exaggerated aspects to it, I am the person you hear on the air. That's me. I had a cat for nine days, and then I sent it to a farm. I knew that if I didn't do it sooner than later, it would be a bigger problem. I love animals, but I love my new condo a little more than animals right now.

By the way, my cat Calisi is still alive. I want to be clear about that. She's literally on a farm, not a "farm" in heaven, but a farm in Virginia. She's got a better life, and I spent almost $400 saving that cat. The last time I saw her, she was roly-poly on a farm, living the fat-cat, happy life. She's doing A-OK. Plus, now I hear that a lot of people are naming their cats Calisi—maybe because of *Game of Thrones*, maybe because that's what I named my cat. Who's to say? I'm a trendsetter.

Aiming to Please

Mike O'Meara

I have spent most of my life trying to please people, starting with my family. Always trying to impress—trying too hard. I get into a room with them and I want to drop the names of people I have interviewed. I want to talk about my accomplishments in radio. It's constant with me.

I can talk to my 93-year-old mom in the assisted living facility in Boston, and it's still, "Mommy, Mommy, look what I did. This is what happened today." All of us, we are all needy.

Robb Spewak

We all need and crave the "attaboy." It doesn't matter from where it comes. It goes back to radio. What are ratings but an affirmation that you're doing your job well?

Mike O'Meara

Even if you're not needy going in, when you get into the meat grinder of a radio station, you're getting a report card regularly. With the advent of Personal People Meters, you're getting ratings once every week. If you weren't screwed up to start with, that'll do the trick.

Robb Spewak

As far as affirmations go, I come from a huge family. I don't know that it has much to do with my parents being divorced except that when my folks split, I was often shuttled off to my grandparents' house. My grandparents had eight kids, and I was essentially the ninth kid, because I was the oldest grandchild.

You've got a mom, a dad, and four kids living at home and the other four kids coming and going. It's a noisy house and it's easy to be overlooked. When you're just a kid, you want attention. I tried to be the loudest, the most talkative, the funniest. I tried to do everything I could to say, "Look at me." I craved attention. I think that's where it started. You get on the air and figure out this is the best way to talk to a lot of people and get a lot of attention.

Oscar Santana

I come from an immigrant family, and when I turned 10 my parents seemed to think I was turning 18. I was left home to fend for myself, left for dead—a latchkey kid. School's over? Time to find a bus ride home, make yourself a PB&J, and answer all sorts of questions for yourself. Questions like: Will I get kidnapped today? Will someone touch me on the Metro? Will I have enough money in my sweaty little hand to get back on the bus by myself since I am fucking 10 years old?

Robb Spewak

Is there a Spanish phrase for "let's roll the dice"?

Oscar Santana

I had to keep reminding them that I was a kid and still needed help, so I guess in that way I was jockeying for their attention.

Robb Spewak

I'm in a constant quest to be liked by everybody, and not just on the radio. This is when I meet people in real life. If someone is standoffish, I want to win them over. I will focus on the one person that does not want to talk to me.

Oscar is brave enough to go out there and say something that he knows is going to make people angry. That is a very strong dividing line between our on-air presences.

Mike O'Meara

After 54 years of life, and much introspection and thought, I've learned that I have to accept this reality: It's not up to other people to value what I do; *I* have to value what I do. I hope I get to the point where other people's opinions just don't matter. Unfortunately, those opinions still matter to me, even though I desperately want them not to.

Robb Spewak

We got into this business for approval, and we need to get past the fact that we're doing it for approval. Will we ever get there? Who knows?

Mike O'Meara

In the movie *On Golden Pond*, Jane Fonda says to Katherine Hepburn, "I'm in charge of Los Angeles. Then I come here, and I feel like a little fat girl." I think we all feel that way to a certain extent. Especially when you are the baby in your family, you can feel inferior. It's a feeling I've always had with my cousins and my sister up in Maine. As the youngest, it can be hard to get the respect that you so desperately want.

Robb Spewak

It makes you want to be the best little fat girl you can be.

Everyone's a Critic

Mike O'Meara

When you do any form of radio, or even the podcast in the show's current incarnation, you're open to public scrutiny. That's it. That's the rules. However, don't believe anybody in the public eye who tells you that criticism doesn't hurt. It hurts, and sometimes it hurts a lot. There are a lot of very nasty people out there, and when they say mean things that are directed at you personally, it can be very hurtful.

Oscar Santana

No one wants to hear negative comments. It sucks. However, I feel like Mike takes things more personally than I do. In my opinion, it has something to do with the generation I grew up in. When Mike started, there was no instant messaging, no forums, no message boards. When I started broadcasting, all of those things were around.

Fans and even radio stations would create message boards, and they were a haven for people to be really positive or really negative about your show. You would find fans who listened and wanted to be part of another "family" of like-minded people. The haters would do the same thing for the same reasons.

Message boards were, and are, places where people can post what they didn't like about a program. Nobody, especially creative people, wants to hear that kind of negativity, but because I've been dealing with it since the beginning of my career, I am sort of used to it. Message boards teach you an important lesson: you can't make everybody happy. However, when the people who don't like what you do are still engaging about your program and talking about it every day, in some sense, that's good enough.

Robb Spewak

I'm a public person by the nature of what I do. If people feel the need to say how horrible I am and how much they hate how I do my job, they have every right to do it. I have glanced at people's rude comments in the past, and I didn't like the way they made me feel, so I stay away from them now. It's not that much different than high school kids getting together and talking about how much they hate certain people at school, but they congregate online because they are protected by a sense of anonymity.

Mike O'Meara

If you're going to take the people that shower you with love and affection all the time, you're going to deal with a little of the crap. I have thousands of friends on my Facebook page, and I have a lovely relationship with most of them. If somebody wants to be a jerk on Facebook, I've got a little button I can press and they're gone. Poof! I don't have to deal with them at all anymore. I enjoy that.

In public forums, we have no control. People can say whatever they want about me or even my family, and there are no consequences. People have no qualms logging on and referring to me as "LFF," which stands for "lazy, fat fuck." When I see that, the hair stands up on the back of my neck and I have to take a deep breath. I have to remind myself that there's nothing I can do about it. When you live in the public eye, you've opened yourself up for criticism.

Robb Spewak

I have news for people who have problems with me on the show: I already know what my problems are. I already know my strengths and weaknesses, so I don't need the "help" identifying them.

Mike O'Meara

Some people live and die by other people's comments. Other people ignore them completely. I am somewhere in the middle. I like to get feedback, to see if there are trends among our listening audience. I want to know if people do and do not like different elements of the show. You take it with a grain of salt. You don't dwell on it; you try to let it go.

You have to remember that the people who write the cruelest things online are also the most cowardly. They cloak themselves in anonymity.

Robb Spewak

People can say anything online, and the nastiest comments are always posted anonymously. People are afraid to put their names on the line—they won't attach themselves to their comments. If they can't be bothered to attach themselves to their own opinions, why should I?

———

Mike O'Meara

When we were let go from WJFK, people were celebrating my firing on some of these radio websites. They love to kick you when you're down. When you get fired from radio, you fail publicly. I lost my job, just like a lot of people lost their jobs during the recession, but everybody and their uncle knew about me getting fired, and a good number of them had opinions about it that they weren't afraid to share with the world.

If you're going to get public adulation, you're going to get public scrutiny. It's a tough world, but it's life; it's the world we live in. It comes with the territory.

Oscar Santana

You'd rather have your ex-girlfriend go on Facebook and say you've got a small penis than fail publicly, at least for me. It's just not fun. No one ever hears your side of the story; they just realize you're not on the radio, so automatically everybody assumes something negative about you.

Mike O'Meara

I've said it before. I tend to focus on the negative, and that can apply to fan feedback. However, with the advent of the podcast, I have received some of the most positive, most supportive feedback ever from fans. If some people like to kick you when you're down, there are other people who will help you back to your feet.

I'll get an email from someone who tells me they're leaving a hospital where their father is dying and the only pleasant moment of their day was when they listened to our show. When someone shares that with you, that's all you need. I think about emails like that a lot, and I am amazed that this little show that we do brings someone that much pleasure, that they can—for an hour and fifteen minutes—forget the horrible circumstances they're living through.

Knowing that our silly show actually helps people ... it's a gift. It gets me up every morning wanting to do the best show I can.

Robb Spewak

The negatives are easily offset by the positives every day. I refuse to take even small things for granted, including something simple like the fact that we're still getting thousands of downloads a day. People don't bother downloading and listening to things they hate. At least not sane people, anyway. The warmth expressed in the kind messages I get on Facebook, in public, in private, and via email makes it much easier to endure the haters.

Mike O'Meara

When I reflect back on my career at the end of my life, it's notes like those that will gratify me. I will not think of the money I used to make as a big-time radio DJ; I won't think about past ratings successes. None of that lasts. What lasts is the generosity of our listeners and how willing they are to share those difficult moments with us.

TMOS Episode #757, Recorded February 14, 2013
Opening Vignette

Mike O'Meara

Greetings, everyone. Welcome to *The Mike O'Meara Show*. Every now and then we throw you a curveball at the beginning of the show. We try to keep the "yuks" rather significant in the opening segment, but every now and then I get correspondence from a listener that throws me for a loop. With his permission, I wanted to share this with you today, because this is something that touches all of us on the show. If you think you're having a bad day today, this may help you realize there are other people who are going through more significant challenges. This comes from my friend Bill Finn on Facebook. It says:

"My family is going through one of the hardest things that we have ever had to do. Our 14-year-old son Tyler has the flu, which led to pneumonia and sepsis. He is currently on life support at the hospital, and he has been for the last three days. It was touch and go, but it finally appears that he may be stable. He is strong and will get through this.

"I just want to thank you for the show. Right now, it is the only thing that I am listening to besides music that Tyler loves. It is keeping a smile on my face, even though this is the worst time of our lives."

I wrote back to him: "Thanks so much, Bill. Your words mean a lot. My prayers go out to your son."

Bill wrote me today, this morning, at 9:45. "I sent you a message last week about my son Tyler, that he was sick with the flu. He passed peacefully yesterday at the hospital. Thank you for your kind response because it meant the world to me.

"For two weeks he was in a coma and all I would listen to was your show. No music, no other shows, just yours. You kept me strong for two weeks and I just want you to know that. Thanks. Bill."

Bill is a sensitive and kind enough guy to share that with us.

Buzz Burbank
Wow, in this moment ...

Mike O'Meara
I wrote this to him today: "I cannot possibly imagine what you are going through right now. Unimaginable pain. I'm the father of a 15- and a 17-year-old. I don't think there is anything I could go through as tough as this. I will have you and your family in my heart as I do the show today, and I will pray that God gives your family the strength to get through this tragedy.

"While no words can adequately help you right now, I have found something to be true when I have experienced great loss in my life. Things will never be the same, but they will get better with time, and the human spirit of your son will live in your hearts forever. I wish you and your family peace, Bill, and for Tyler, I hope he is in a place where all of his dreams are reality ..."

A long pause ensues as Mike's emotions swell and he fights to control them.

Mike O'Meara
"... and he is welcomed into a place more beautiful than any of us could ever dream of."

I asked his permission to share this, but to get this message first thing this morning, I just want to say to Bill and to your family, our thoughts go out to you. I can't imagine what it is like to lose a 14-year-old to pneumonia.

I don't know you, Bill, and I didn't know Tyler. I don't know your wife, Tonya. I don't know your other son Eric, who is 5 years old. Just know that for his send-off today, I have come around spiritually to the power of prayer, so if we get everybody associated with this show to pray for your son, that will get him to a better place. Start the show.

Buzz Burbank
Amen. ∎

———

Bill Finn (Listener and Father of Tyler)
My son died from the flu, even though he had his flu shot and probably should have been fine. He was put on life support right away when he got to the hospital. My wife stayed with him most of the time, but I still had to take care of our house and go to work. I would drive back and forth but I would only listen to *TMOS*. It was getting me through this very hard time, and I cannot even begin to explain how much it helped me cope with this terrible situation.

Mike opened that Valentine's Day show with Tyler's story. It was one of the few times I ever heard the show open without a comedy bit. I still go back and watch that show on YouTube every once in a while, but it is very hard because I start crying. It meant the world to me and my family that they would put this on the air. It shows just how much he cares and truly does wear his heart on his sleeve.

10

THE BEGINNING

This book began at "the end" of *TMOS*, on the day Mike, Robb, and Oscar lost their radio jobs. However, that corporate decision did not end the show. That end was a door to a new beginning. While the group was finally starting to believe they had found a new broadcasting home online, the last brick in that new home was their first live show at the State Theater in Falls Church, Virginia.

They'd spent months cocooned in a living room studio, knowing that people were listening to the show but unable to interact with the audience. Most people listen to podcasts asynchronously, whenever the time best fits their schedules. Aside from the prohibitive cost of installing dedicated phone lines and figuring out how to wire them into their ad hoc system, there was no real use in opening phone lines for callers. Most people would be listening hours or days later.

For DJs who had spent years taking hundreds of phone calls from listeners live on the air every week, a podcast was an isolated life. Each day they recorded a show, uploaded it to a server, and left the studio in silence, hoping people would listen to the work they'd completed. They did receive some feedback, usually through public and private Facebook messages, but this type of listener feedback was almost as foreign as the podcasting medium they'd landed in. It wasn't immediate, and it was impersonal in the same way a text message from a friend just isn't the same as a phone call.

It would take a live show, in front of hundreds of live listeners, for them to grasp how the show was not only alive but thriving.

Mystery Guest

Mike O'Meara

Big O and Dukes held a live show at the State Theater after we started our podcast, and they invited me to come on stage with them.

Oscar Santana

The live show was in March 2011. You were our mystery guest!

Mike O'Meara

I was nervous to go out there, because I'd always worried that the *Big O and Dukes* audience would look at me with suspicious eyes when I came into the room: "What are *you* doing here?" I had no idea I'd get the reception I got. I don't think Oscar and Chad knew what kind of reception I'd get either.

However, they were so generous to offer me the chance to come out, I had to do it. I also felt like this would be a really good way of getting closure with Chad. He'd basically taken my afternoon slot at WJFK after I left. That was initially very tough for me, and it took me some time to get over. Coming to their live show was my way of burying the hatchet. Chad and I are still on good terms to this day.

Oscar Santana

Think about it from my end. I'd worked with Chad for almost eight years. I was lucky enough to start working with Mike, and on both ends, there was a lack of communication. Mike's doing afternoons on WJFK and then Chad getting that time slot ... Mike and I looked at it differently. From my perspective, it turned into a sports station instead of a hot talk station. From Mike's perspective, it's still afternoons on 106.7. Once he came out on stage and saw how the shows and their listeners support each other, it made it easier for me.

Mike O'Meara

Oscar's brought a lot of people from that show, behind-the-scenes personnel like our engineer Pony Boy, to *TMOS*. I get a feeling that there's a small segment of the listening audience that wants radio warfare, but there's a much, much greater segment that would rather have peace.

Anyway, I was so enamored of that experience that I immediately wanted to steal it, like any great idea in radio. We did our show at the State Theater a year later. We put tickets up for sale, and I didn't know whether they would sell or not. Oscar was pretty confident that they would.

Robb Spewak

Oscar is always confident.

Mike O'Meara

Everything is "amazing" and "great" with Oscar.

Robb Spewak

I wasn't all that confident ...

Oscar Santana

Hey! When do I not deliver? I always deliver!

Robb Spewak

One thing I remember leading up to the show was needing to sell "this many" tickets to make the evening work, to make it worthwhile doing.

Mike O'Meara

It was 400 tickets to make it work, and everything above and beyond that would be really successful.

Robb Spewak

And then we could open up more space at the theater as tickets sold.

Oscar Santana

800 tickets meant a total sellout.

Robb Spewak

Selling between 400 and 800 tickets? No, I was not confident. I've seen Mike bring out tremendous crowds for free promotional events, especially back in *The Don and Mike Show* days, but never for a paying event. This was the first time we charged for tickets.

Mike O'Meara

Because of our financial reality, this is the way we make our living. It was a leap, because when we were sponsored by a radio station, we did free appearances. Everybody did free appearances. Disc jockeys didn't get ticket sales to go out and do stand-up. Comedians did.

We were basically asking people to pay to come see a show we usually do for free online. We had no idea if it would succeed. We had no idea if people would respond to it, but they did. People clamored for it, and we sold out the whole damn joint.

Robb Spewak

It sold out in a couple of weeks, faster than we'd hoped. Mike and I shared a pretty great moment, because we were nervous up until the time we took the stage. We were up in a horrible dressing room that had a dirty, open window.

We could see that the line to get in the theater snaked around from the front of the building to the back alley. We could hear the echoes of people in the alley, waiting to get in, reciting bits from the show *en masse*. We heard a chorus of 50 people doing a Scott Shannon Life Savers commercial that we used to riff on.

Mike O'Meara

[In a very affected DJ voice] Are you in the market for some delicious candy?

Robb Spewak

[In a similarly schlocky DJ voice] What kind of candy?

Mike O'Meara

How about Life Savers candy?

Robb Spewak

But what flavor?

Mike O'Meara

Wint-o-green.

Robb Spewak

Pep-o-mint.

Mike O'Meara and Robb Spewak (unison)

And traditional five-flavors.

Mike O'Meara

We knew they were into the show. That moment alone told us so much. That was enough to know that the podcast was going to succeed. Right there—that was enough.

Robb Spewak

It was a turning point for us.

Carla O'Meara

The guys were shocked by the listener response. I got to watch their reactions as the tickets sold as quickly as they did. "Carla, we sold 20 more tickets! Carla, we sold 400 tickets and sold out the first level of the theater!" They were like little kids on Christmas Day. Just seeing the thrill on Mike's face when all of the tickets sold out was incredible. It gave them a boost of confidence exactly when they needed it most.

Mike O'Meara

I remember saying to myself, "This is real. This is real."

Oscar Santana

You dedicate your life to do the program you want to do on your own terms ...

Mike O'Meara

... And to have it be received that way was incredible. We knew if we had a core that was this loyal, we could build on that and continue to keep building it. The live show was definitely a moment where I truly believed that the podcast was a viable business model.

Oscar Santana

Something you also realize, especially at the first show, is that not only are people willing to come out and support the show, but everybody is there for the right reasons. Those are the people who are listening every day. It's not just the $20 they spend to buy a ticket. They want to help build and sustain what's on the stage. It's like your family's there, and your family's rooting for you. There's no better feeling than that.

Robb Spewak

There have been so many times that I have left the living room and my stomach hurts because I have been laughing for an hour. Every day, I get to do something I love for a living. I get paid to crack jokes and be a pain in the ass. You know what they say: "Find something you love doing and you'll never work a day in your life." I went to school with people who are doctors and lawyers and some of them hate their jobs, even if they make a lot of money. Some of them dread going to work. I don't. I get excited every day.

I've got a 45-minute drive to Mike's house. He has to come down the stairs, which is also a tough commute, I guess. I drive for 45 minutes. When I get to Manassas and I see the used tire stores, car dealerships, and the bowling store, I get excited! I know that I am a half-hour away from sitting down with some really funny people.

I get excited about it every day. I got excited about it today. I love it. However, it's really not a polite way to make a living, because it is mostly based on farts.

Oscar Santana

I feel like I won the lottery, that I get to come here and do this for a living—pay my mortgage and get to work with these guys. It certainly has made me a better broadcaster. You could walk into a Fortune 500 company and ask how many people actually like their jobs. I'd bet it's not many.

Some of them make amazing livings and don't have to worry about money, but they're not nearly as happy as I am. I feel like I am lucky to do this, I think all of us realize how lucky we are, even Mike. His constant bitching is just who he is so ignore that.

Robb Spewak

My wife works as a manager at a retail store. Every morning when she wakes up and every evening when she goes to bed she worries. She worries that people will do their jobs. We've never had that worry here. We're a team, and we're equal partners in this venture.

Mike Kelley

I'm thinking about the juxtaposition of when, recently, Robb's wife is posting on Facebook that she's sitting in the parking lot outside of her job crying because she has to face another day working there. Robb, does it ever make you feel bad that your wife is so unhappy while you are so happy at work?

Robb Spewak

At times.

Oscar Santana

He means "never."

Mike O'Meara

He comes in and high-fives us every morning. "She's going to have another shitty day today! Yes!"

Robb Spewak

Well I have to find happiness somewhere, don't I, Mike? Seriously, though, a day doesn't pass where I don't relish the stars aligning to bring *TMOS* to life as a podcast. We've landed where we should be. There are people who go through a lifetime and never get to land where they should be.

Mike O'Meara

The difference between now and the way it's always been is that I love the work now. I wish I knew better how to relish the good while I'm in it, to really appreciate what we've done here in a living room studio. I don't know how it all came together, looking back, but it's been the greatest rush and the happiest I've been in my broadcasting career.

Afterword
My Former Radio Partners
By Mike O'Meara

One of the toughest things during a career in the public eye is any type of failure, personal or professional. I have been blessed to have a good many success stories throughout my 30 plus years in the business of show. Listeners have also been with me during my sad times, divorce, loss of loved ones, and layoffs. I look back on my years in this business with no regrets. I believe that everything that happened in my life happened for a reason, and no matter what the story, nothing really matters when you look at the big picture.

A lot has been made of my relationship with Don Geronimo. Folks like to talk about a "rift" or "bad blood." The fact is that Don and I went through a great deal together, good times and bad. At a certain time in Don's life, he chose to move on from the old *Don and Mike Show*. We had a tremendous 20-year run, which is a lifetime in the radio business.

At first when Don started doing other radio shows without me, I was hurt. I wondered why he would want to get out of our remarkably successful partnership and then jump right back into another radio situation so soon after leaving our show. As the years have gone by, I have reflected on this often, and I have come up with one solid truth: I am not Don Geronimo. Don suffered publicly in a way I haven't. I can't project what my emotions and thoughts would be if I were him. I would never try to speak for him or explain his actions.

I will say that I was sad that our partnership ended in such an unsettled way. There were many things in my professional relationship with Don that I wish had been different, but that may have been what made us successful in the first place. We had a terrific run, and he taught me so much. We also fought some terrific battles together and, in the end, we can look back with pride on an association that hopefully made a significant mark in the radio business.

The truth is, as of this writing, we are not particularly close. We have both moved on, and Don, after many years in radio, is diving into podcasting. Sometimes you cannot explain why a distance becomes greater between people, and in our business in particular, separations create a vast array of emotions. I think of Don often, and I wish him true happiness. If our paths ever cross again, the first thing I would do would be to give him a big hug.

We are very different people, but we are also alike in many ways; one of those is our competitiveness. I think that is what made us winners, but it also may have contributed to our distance in the end. I wish him nothing but the greatest happiness in his life, and I thank him for an incredible time in my career.

There have been other professional relationships over the years that have ended, and I would be lying if I didn't say that feelings sometimes get hurt when people move on. But in the end, you move on as well, and you keep on working. You really don't have a choice. I am blessed to be doing something I love to do. I really didn't know how much I loved doing a show until I started *TMOS*. All of the people I have worked with have had their own special gifts, and I wouldn't change any of it.

158

When it comes to *TMOS*, the original cast was me, Robb Spewak, Oscar Santana, and Buzz Burbank. Buzz left the show in 2013 along with our business manager, Marc Ronick. Although I was sad to see Buzz leave, I hope he is happy and that he continues to enjoy doing what he loves to do.

My show with Robb and Oscar has been the most fun I have ever had in my career. With no disrespect to Buzz, things changed dramatically after he left. Having only three guys flapping their gums every day streamlined the show in a way that I never thought possible. I now describe the show as "three guys busting each other's balls," but it is so much more than that. Oscar and Robb contribute so much to the show both on and off the air, and I have enjoyed every minute of our partnership.

Robb Spewak, at least when I'm around him, is always "on." He doesn't stop. When we're on the road somewhere, that is incredible to me. I will never, ever travel with anyone who brings me as much joy as Robb Spewak. Robb has managed to take his passions in life and weave them into his career, and the love that he has for life and his family is something that I admire every day.

Oscar Santana never seems to slow down either, but in a much different way than Robb. Oscar's dedication to the business side of *TMOS*, as well as his daily contribution to the show itself, has been incredible to watch. Oscar is always thinking, learning, and creating. Recently, since research for this book concluded, I have moved out of my home in Virginia and moved to Florida. We now broadcast from multiple living rooms, and Oscar has made that possible. I will always be grateful to him for that. Oscar, too, has so much love for his family, and I think, ultimately, that love for the people who are close to us may be the true bond that the three of us share. I hope we all can work together for a very long time.

In our business, change is a given. People come and go more than in other businesses, and because this is also a competitive world, it sometimes takes time for the dust to settle after turnover occurs. In the end, you have to let things go. You have to move on with your life, and you have to key in on what is happening in the moment. If you focus on the past and worry about the future you will forget to enjoy what you are doing right now.

Do I like everybody I have ever worked with? Of course I don't, but I realize that everyone has to deal with their own issues, and everybody wants to make a living. I think it would be ludicrous to slam any of the people I have worked with in the past, because they have contributed to where I am right now. I know I have contributed to where they are in their lives.

In the end, when we're all old and blowing spit bubbles, I hope I can remember the good things about all of my coworkers. I hope they will do the same for me. Everybody has a different story, and only they know how that story affects them. I think everybody wants to find their special place, and some folks do a better job of it than others. The key is to keep on moving and to focus on the person who really matters: you.

Mike O'Meara
April 2014

If you enjoyed this book, please consider reading another of our titles based on *The Mike O'Meara Show*:

These Boots Were Made for Fighting

The Jibrils of Madison County

Men Are From Mars, Women Are From A Place Where I Break Your Computer and Sunglasses

Bad Dog! Shaming Your Chihuahua to Cure its Fecal Incontinence

The Very Hungry Spewak

Butterfly, Grounded: Literacy and the Modern ESOL Student

Made in the USA
Lexington, KY
10 June 2014